THE
PAPER HAT
BOOK

THE
PAPER HAT
BOOK

Super Hats for Super Kids

ALYN CARLSON

FOREWORD BY AMY AZZARITO

Quarry Books
100 Cummings Center, Suite 406L
Beverly, MA 01915

quarrybooks.com • craftside.typepad.com

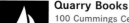

For Levi and Wallace, who continue to teach their Mippy how to play

First published in the United States of America by
Quarry Books, a member of
Quarto Publishing Group USA Inc.
100 Cummings Center
Suite 406-L
Beverly, Massachusetts 01915-6101
Telephone: (978) 282-9590
Fax: (978) 283-2742
www.quarrybooks.com
Visit www.Craftside.Typepad.com for a behind-the-scenes peek at our crafty world!

Library of Congress Cataloging-in-Publication Data

Carlson, Alyn.
  The paper hat book : super hats for super kids / by Alyn Carlson ; foreword by Amy Azzarito.
    pages cm
  ISBN 978-1-59253-940-6 (paperback)
  1. Paper hat making. I. Title.
  TT870.C258 2014
  745.59--dc23

                                                    2014004610

ISBN: 978-1-59253-940-6

Digital edition published in 2014
eISBN: 978-1-62788-214-9

10 9 8 7 6 5 4 3 2 1

Design: Rita Sowins / Sowins Design
Photography: Paul Clancy
Templates: Alyn Carlson

Printed in China

Contents

Foreword

BY AMY AZZARITO OF DESIGN*SPONGE

In 2009, I wrote a blog post for design*sponge, a design and lifestyle blog. It was only my second for the site, and it featured Alyn's home. Nearly five years and hundreds of home tours later, Alyn's home still stands out and remains one of my favorites.

The post was also a favorite with readers, and it received more than 100 comments. I think it resonated with both our readers and me because the home was filled with examples of Alyn's boundless creativity and enthusiasm for creating. That enthusiasm is something that she captures here, within the pages of this book.

Alyn is not a solitary artist working in a garret somewhere. For her, creating is about sharing knowledge, and she is certainly knowledgeable when it comes to creating with paper. Her years and years of work with paper have been solidified and refined within each set of instructions, making them easy to understand and adapt.

This book is guaranteed to create a new generation of paper artists. Whether you're searching for the perfect Halloween costume or just want to liven up a birthday party, this is the book for you.

Introduction

I LOVE HATS. Lids, crowns, fedoras, berets, caps, sombreros, toppers, cloches, stovepipes, bowlers, bonnets, fascinators, tams, babushkas, boaters, duckbills, and baker boy caps—I love them all. People often say I look good in hats, and they wish they did, too. I feel there's a hat shape for everyone, but most of the time adults are too self-conscious to wear one.

That's not the case with children. They know that a hat can transform the person who wears it into someone else, if only for a moment. Hats provide a great excuse to play, make up a story, pretend to live in a faraway place long ago, or even be from another planet. Kids also know that wearing a hat can make them feel more special or important.

My parents are both artists and I was lucky to grow up in a home where creativity was encouraged. If you could imagine it, you could draw it, and if you could draw it, you could make it. I learned about color and how to draw from my father, a painter and illustrator. I learned sewing and garment construction from my mother, a seamstress. Some of my earliest memories involve helping my parents with creative projects, and often I learned just by watching them work.

Halloween was the show-stopper in our family. My three sisters and I relished the experience and power of disappearing inside of a costume for a night. To create our costumes, we may have needed to run out and purchase a particular color of yarn or a special prop, but we could easily forage most of the ingredients from household items or from the woods behind our house.

With my children and grandchildren, I've carried on the tradition of costume making for Halloween and everyday play. We search for and creatively transform materials from around the house. My love of paper, especially found paper, has lead me to create hats as pieces of art as well as play.

I've written the instructions in this book in hopes that you'll include the child for whom the hat is intended in the creative process. Please think of my designs, which were inspired by my young friends who are wearing them in the photographs, as a starting point. I encourage you to change and alter these designs according to your child's imagination and materials you find along the way.

CHAPTER 1

Getting STARTED

Sources of Inspiration

As you work on these projects, feel free to choose materials similar to what is used in the projects featured in this book or create something that is uniquely yours. Watch for colors, patterns, and textures that work well together and sometimes surprise. You can find these combinations in nature, fashion history, cultural celebrations, your closet, a poster, or even the cereal aisle at the grocery store.

As a designer and artist who spends a lot of time at my computer, I look online for great ideas. I'm a frequent visitor to Pinterest, Etsy, and design*sponge. But I often find that I discover the best and most surprising sources for inspiration when I go through simple everyday activities, such as taking a walk, visiting a museum, or opening a book. Bringing a child along on an excursion often opens up even more possibilities.

INSPIRATION IN NATURE

Get outside and go for a walk or visit a park. Observe any birds, plants, underwater creatures, landscapes, weather, shells, and insects you see. Use the fabulous colors, textures, and design combinations found in the natural world to inspire your designs.

INSPIRATION IN FASHION

Go window shopping or visit a museum exhibit. New runway styles, traditional folk costume, royalty wear, historic fashion, and tribal costume are fun resources.

INSPIRATION IN PATTERN

Plan a trip to the library to explore books about quilts, wallpaper patterns, furniture, painted china, and textiles, especially those from Japan, Scandinavia, Africa, China, and South America. Exploring patterns is one of my favorite ways to find the inspiration for a hat.

INSPIRATION IN PRINTED MATTER

Antique shops, old bookstores, and flea markets offer a variety of ephemera to purchase or use for study.

Paper

You can find all kinds of free and purchased papers that work well for paper hat making. Because of the weight and texture, some papers work better for a hat base while others work well for embellishment.

PAPER FOR HAT BASES

The type of paper you're looking for depends upon the type of hat you're making.

HEADBANDS: Heavy brown craft paper, such as the paper used to make grocery bags, is recommended.

FOLDED BOAT HATS: This is a fun rainy-day classic that's usually made from newspaper. Kraft paper or other paper that is similar in weight and opacity can also be used. An outdated map or old wallpaper samples, for example, are also perfect for this design.

CONE HATS AND BRIM HATS: Depending on the design, you'll need a cover weight for cone hats, and a lighter weight, less opaque paper for brim hats. Cover weight feels like a business or greeting card. If you hold it up to the light, it will be opaque. It comes with a coated surface, which is a little shiny, or an uncoated surface, which is a little dull. I tend to prefer uncoated, because it's sometimes easier to recycle and looks more earth friendly. I recommend using cover stock if you are making a hat that requires the strength to stand up, such as the Wee Bunny (see page 89) or the Can O'Worms (see page 116) styles.

Lighter weight craft shopping bags, the type that don't have constructed bottoms and handles, are ideal for soft-brim styles. You can easily fold, pinch, or gather this paper into any shape you want. Other good examples of lighter weight papers are newsprint, wrapping paper, or packaging paper—the large, wrinkled sheets of perforated or soft craft paper used to protect fragile items during shipping.

BUYING PAPER

You can buy coated or dull cover stock and light craft paper at local or online art supply, craft, or department stores for a reasonable price. Sold in large (19" x 24" [48.5 x 61 cm]) pads, the cover stock is sometimes called Bristol. Light craft comes in large pads or rolls.

Your local grocery, art, craft, and office supply stores also sell lots of paper options, such as tissue paper, wax paper, bubble wrap, paper plates, cupcake liners, parchment baking paper, gift wrap, paper lawn bags, freezer paper, construction paper, paper tablecloths and napkins, Sudoku or crossword puzzle books, straws, paper tags, sticky notes, silk screened paper, graph paper, neon copy paper, and specialty printed papers. Flea markets, library sales, thrift shops, and used bookstores are great places to buy comic books, maps, colorful cookbooks, and children's books.

Look a little further, and it's easy to get lost looking at papers from all over the world that are available online or in stores. Some affordable options include paper from China, India, Japan, and Italy.

Joss paper, which is also called ghost money, comes from China. It's printed in bright reds and metallic gold. A light, soft paper, it's made especially to be burned at funerals and special occasions.

Hand printed and rolled papers from India can be fun to layer, adding a nice texture to a hat.

Origami paper from Japan comes in small, medium, and large squares. It's printed in solid colors, with metallic inks, and in patterns. Different patterns can represent different ideas, such as good fortune, beauty, or a long life.

Papers from Italy are printed with delicate, Florentine patterns or marbled motifs, sometimes with touches of metallic gold. The Italian tradition of printing fine papers dates back to the Renaissance.

FINDING FREE PAPER

You may have a printing company in your local area. They are a great source for free, recycled cover-weight paper. Often after a print run, stacks of large colorfully printed paper goes to recycling because of imperfections. I've found many printing companies love the idea of people using their leftovers for art projects.

Most of us occasionally forget to bring cloth bags for grocery shopping. The nice stash of grocery shopping bags that accumulate are perfect for making headband and some brim hats.

You can often find free sources of paper to use as embellishments, which add creative flair, a sense of fashion, and personality to every hat you make. The possibilities are as endless as your amazing imagination.

It's fun to be on the lookout for free paper to embellish your hat and make it one of a kind. Junk mail envelopes, cereal boxes, event postcards and posters, gum wrappers, magazines, seed packages, outdated maps, old story books, recipe cards, stamps, toilet and paper towel rolls, old photos, shoe boxes, comics, bubble wrap, paint chips, board game money, sheet music, store circulars, take-out menus, holiday cards, bakery bags, egg cartons, flour and sugar bags, calendars, telephone books, mesh produce bags, ski lift tags, movie and concert ticket stubs, catalogues, soup labels, coloring books, notebooks, and even old homework can all be upcycled into artful hats.

Techniques

Here are a few basic paper craft techniques that will help you make the projects in this book.

FOLDING AND CREASING

Papers respond to folding in different ways. Heavier or thicker papers will produce a deeper, more defined crease or fold. Lighter papers will make a less defined fold. Ephemera or antique papers don't take a fold very well unless they are backed with a heavier paper.

Keep in mind that, like fabric, most papers have a grain to them. If you fold the paper with the grain, it will give you a smoother crease. The grain usually runs top to bottom. By gently bending you can determine if the crease will be smooth or jagged.

When you are folding paper, to create a smoother fold, you can score the paper with the rounded curve of a paperclip along a metal ruler.

CURLING AND CRIMPING

To curl paper, I use a smooth pencil or dowel. The smaller the diameter of the dowel, the tighter the curl.

I crimp paper by folding accordion-style, making folds ¼ to ½ inch (6 to 13 mm) from each other. I encourage you to try different widths, to see what you like best.

FANNING

This works best with a half or quarter page of paper, folding from a center point in one corner to the outer edges. I trim when the fan is folded, making a decorative, curved, or pointed edge on each wedge.

Basic Tools

The following tools will help you to make these projects more quickly and efficiently.

CUTTING TOOLS

You can buy these tools online and at most craft stores.

PAPER SCISSORS

I recommend never using sewing scissors to cut paper because the blades will become extremely dull. Fabric sheers are usually more expensive, and they are labeled "for sewing." Instead, buy a pair of scissors that are made for cutting paper. Craft stores offer a wide range of affordable scissors.

CUTTING MAT

I recommend a self-healing mat, which is the type used by graphic designers and quilters. These are printed with measured lines, which makes things easier. Buy a good size mat because you may be cutting paper as large 26" (66 cm).

PAPER TRIMMER

There are basically two styles of paper trimmers in lots of different sizes and price points. I've used both the gulliotine-style paper cutters and rotary trimmer cutters, and both get the job done. I prefer the rotary style, and have a RotaTrim, which cuts very accurately and saves so much time when cutting lots of small pieces of paper, such as petals or tendrils.

SMALL SHARP SCISSORS

A pair with a tip small enough to make tiny holes is handy for attaching flowers and elastic thread.

PINKING SHEARS, DECORATIVE EDGE SCISSORS, OR SPECIAL DIE-CUTTERS

Craft stores carry sets of decorative scissors that are lightweight and handy for quickly giving a flower leaf or brim edge a much more interesting look. You can also buy decorative die-cut hole punches to cut elaborate shapes such as snowflakes, lace edges, or flowers. I have two that I bought on sale, and they work best on text-weight paper, which is the same as copier paper. Heavier stock tends to clog them.

CRAFT KNIFE

This type of knife works best when partnered with a cork-backed stainless steel ruler (see below). Keep lots of blades handy because this tool works best when it's nice and sharp.

MEASURING TOOLS

Most of these tools are also sold online and at craft stores, or they can be found around your home.

CORK-BACKED STAINLESS STEEL RULER

One that is 24" (61 cm) will work for most of these projects. The cork back keeps the ruler from slipping.

MEASURING TAPE

The cloth or plastic measuring tapes that are commonly used for sewing work best for hat making.

WELL-SHARPENED HARD AND SOFT PENCILS

A hard pencil (2H, 4H, 6H) is nice for making small measured marks, while a soft pencil (2B, 4B, 6B) is best for making long marks that need to be erased.

CIRCLE TEMPLATES

These can be purchased at stores that carry quilting supplies, or look around the house for thread spools, mixing bowls, and coffee cups.

GLUING OR ATTACHING TOOLS

Most of these tools are sold online and at craft stores, too.

HOT GLUE GUN

I've tried the cold glue version and have had bad results. Hot glue seems to bond better. You will go through a lot of glue sticks, so make sure you have plenty on hand before you begin.

SPRAY GLUE

I use this occasionally on large, flat surfaces, such as brims and sides of hats. It's sold in different strengths, and I use a more heavy-duty version. Make sure you spray glue in a well-ventilated area and burnish it well, pushing air bubbles from the center, out to edges.

BURNISHERS

Burnishers, which ensure a good bond between papers and spray glue, come in different shapes and sizes: flat, wide, curved, and with round tips. Cover the paper you're burnishing with a sheet of tracing paper and then use the burnisher to press firmly and smoothly over the whole surface. You can buy these in craft or art supply stores, or you can use anything that has a large flat plastic surface, such as a plastic triangle.

SEWING MACHINE

Believe it or not, you can easily stitch paper together with a sewing machine. I've made many hats that were held together with stitching and very little glue. Experiment on some scrap paper first, setting the tension so that it is not too tight nor too loose.

TAPE

½" or 1" (1.3 cm or 2.5 cm) masking or white art tape is handy when piecing small sheets of paper together.

ELASTIC THREAD

I've tried different weights of elastic thread for cone hats, and I've found 2.7 mm works best. For the sake of comfort, I also put the attached elastic under the child's hair instead of under the chin.

HELPFUL, OPTIONAL TOOLS

A few of the hats in this book call for special tools, such as a large darning needle, a smooth round pencil or small dowel, watercolor paint set, watercolor or wax crayons, single hole punch, and floral tape and wire. I also use small- and medium-size bulldog clips and wooden clothespins to hold pieces together while I'm fitting or gluing. Sometimes I decorate my hat while it sits on a hat stand. You can make your own hat stand by balling up newspaper to the size of your child's head, covering with a smooth sheet, and taping it to a weighted candlestick or vase.

CHAPTER 2

Headband
HATS

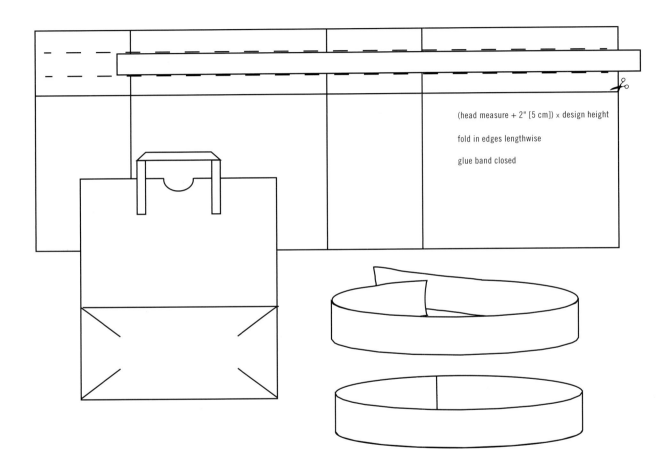

(head measure + 2" [5 cm]) × design height

fold in edges lengthwise

glue band closed

measure to fit head, overlap ends, and glue

Headband Base Construction

{ MATERIALS }

» PAPER GROCERY BAG, large enough to yield a piece of paper that is at least 2" (5 cm) longer than the circumference of your head and double the height required for the design.

» PENCIL

» RULER

» SCISSORS

» HOT GLUE GUN AND GLUE

INSTRUCTIONS

1. Lengthwise on the paper, use a pencil and ruler to draw a rectangle that measures the circumference of your head plus 2" (5 cm) wide × hat design height.

2. Cut out the rectangle and place it horizontally in front of you. Fold the top and bottom edges in by 1½" (4 cm).

3. Inside the folded edges, run a thin line of glue and carefully fold the band shut, while smoothing out the edges.

4. When assembly of the hat is complete, wrap the band around the head of the intended wearer, overlapping the ends to fit. Use a pencil to mark where the band should end. Trim off any excess band if necessary. Remove the band from the wearer. Apply glue under the overlap and press down to secure. Allow the glue to dry before wearing.

Floral Flapper

Flappers, who were known for their fabulous dance moves, needed hats that stayed on their heads. This floral headband can turn a birthday party into a flapper bash.

I found a Marimekko pattern printed on newspaper reminiscent of Japanese fabrics, which were popular during the Roaring Twenties. I've used it for color inspiration and as material for some flowers.

To find more inspiration for your own unique creation, look up famous flappers Anita Page, Clara Bow, Josephine Baker, Louise Brooks, and Zelda Fitzgerald.

Designers of the 1920s who created the fabulous flapper look were Coco Chanel, Paul Poiret, Elsa Schiaparelli, and Jean Patou.

NOTE: Some of the embellishments commonly used to dress up flapper hats were feathers, strings of beads, flowers, pom-poms, netting, ribbon, pearls, embroidery, and tassels.

{ MATERIALS }

- » **A:** BRIGHT PINK COVER-WEIGHT PAPER TO MATCH THE PATTERNED NEWSPRINT
- » **B:** BRIGHT TEAL COVER-WEIGHT PAPER TO MATCH THE PATTERNED NEWSPRINT
- » **C:** BRIGHT LIME GREEN PRINTED ON A GROCERY BAG
- » **D:** BRIGHT CORAL TEXT-WEIGHT PAPER
- » **E:** SOFT GREEN RIBBED COVER-WEIGHT PAPER
- » **F:** LIGHT GREY COVER-WEIGHT PAPER
- » **G:** 8" x 8" (20.5 x 20.5 CM) SQUARE NEWSPRINT PAPER WITH COLORFUL PATTERN
- » 2 WHITE PAPER MINI CUPCAKE LINERS
- » CIRCLE TEMPLATES MEASURING 1" (2.5 CM), 1½" (4 CM), 2" (5 CM), 2½" (6.5 CM), AND 3" (7.5 CM)
- » PENCIL
- » SCISSORS
- » HOT GLUE GUN AND GLUE

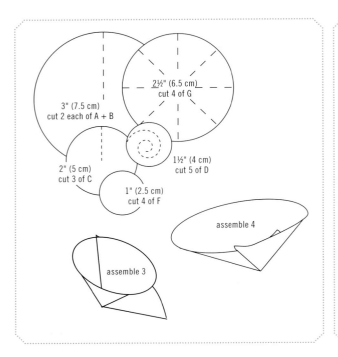

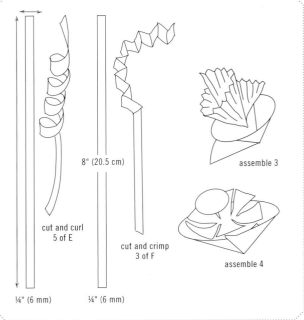

INSTRUCTIONS

FLOWERS

1. Using a 3" (7.5 cm) circle template, trace and cut two circles from A and B and, using a 2" (5 cm) circle template, cut three circles from C.
2. Cut a slit from the outer edge to the middle of each circle made with A and B. Pull and overlap the cut slit edges (about 1½" [4 cm]) and glue to form a cone.
3. Repeat step 2 with circles made using C, but overlap 3" (7.5 cm) to form a cone with leaf.
4. Using a 1½" (4 cm) circle template, trace and cut five circles from D. Cut a spiral in each of the paper circles made with D.

VINES

1. Cut five ¼" (6 mm) strips 8" (20.5 cm) long from E. Curl each tightly around a pencil to form a spiral.
2. Cut three ¼" (6 mm) strips 8" (20.5 cm) long from F. Half the length of the strip and make small crimped folds.

3. Cut 4 circles 2½" (6.5 cm) wide using G. Cut 8 slits from outer edge to center, taking care to leave some of the center whole. Glue centers of G to centers of paper cones made using A and B.
4. Cut four small circles 1" (2.5 cm) wide from F and glue the center of each to cones made using A and B.
5. Cut the small cupcake liners in half, roll into a slight spiral, and glue into paper cones made with C.

HAT BASE

1. Using a paper grocery bag, follow step 1 for Headband Base Construction on page 31, making the band height 6" (15 cm). Fold in half horizontally and glue along open edge.
2. Place the band in front of you horizontally and fold the entire band in half from left to right. Leave the band folded and use a pencil to lightly mark the center.
3. Then, beginning at the end of the band, measure 1½" (4 cm) up from the bottom edge and mark lightly with a pencil. Draw a curve to join the mark made 1½" (4 cm) up on the end to the top edge at the center fold. You can draw this curve freehand, or trace it using a flexible curve or the top edge of a large bowl.
4. Trim along the curve and use hot glue to secure the edge just cut. The widest part of the band is the hat front.

ASSEMBLE

1. Using hot glue, attach the large paper flowers to the hat front, left of center, alternating colors.
2. Glue small paper flowers above, below, and to the sides of the large flowers. Glue spiral vines on top and bottom, to far the left of flowers and crimped vines below.
3. To adjust the band size, follow step 4 in Headband Base Construction on page 31.

Super Hero

Because I used silver, this hat could also work for a medieval knight's helmet.

Both a super hero and knight like to conceal their identity while fighting for the underdog, so this hat can be worn with a homemade or party store eye mask. I used recycled aluminum foil with a flash of cupcake liner to give our super hero a strong-as-steel look. You could also make armor from egg cartons, a colorful cereal box, or a shiny black shoebox.

{ MATERIALS }

» **A:** 8½" x 11" (21.5 x 28 CM) SILVER METALLIC PAPER
» **B:** 8½" x 11" (21.5 x 28 CM) GREY/BLUE CARD STOCK
» **C:** 8½" x 11" (21.5 x 28 CM) BLUE/GREY MOTTLED METALLIC PAPER
» **D:** 2" x 2" (5 x 5 CM) BLACK AND GREY PATTERNED PAPER
» **E:** SILVER CUPCAKE LINER, REGULAR SIZE
» PENCIL
» SCISSORS
» SPRAY GLUE
» HOT GLUE GUN AND GLUE

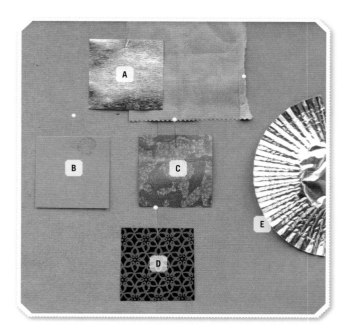

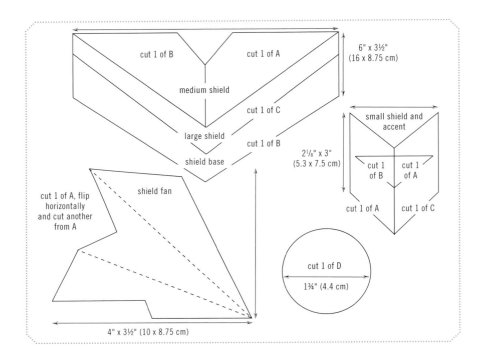

The figure shows cutting templates with the following labels:

- cut 1 of B / medium shield / cut 1 of A
- 6" x 3½" (16 x 8.75 cm)
- large shield / cut 1 of C
- shield base / cut 1 of B
- cut 1 of A, flip horizontally and cut another from A
- shield fan
- small shield and accent
- 2⅛" x 3" (5.3 x 7.5 cm)
- cut 1 of B / cut 1 of A
- cut 1 of A / cut 1 of C
- cut 1 of D
- 1¾" (4.4 cm)
- 4" x 3½" (10 x 8.75 cm)

INSTRUCTIONS

ARROWHEADS, SHIELD, AND FAN

1. Using templates, trace and cut a fan from paper A. Flip the pattern horizontally and cut another from A.

2. Trace and cut the right side of the medium shield and accent from A.

3. Trace and cut the shield base, left side of medium base, and left side of accent from B. Score and fold the shield base vertically.

4. Cut the large shield and right side of small shield from C. Score and fold small the shield vertically.

5. Using pinking shears, cut a circle from D.

6. Gently flatten the cupcake liner, leaving ridges intact, and spray glue the center circle D to liner E.

HAT BASE

1. Using a paper grocery bag, follow steps 1–3 for Headband Base Construction on page 31, making the total band height 6" (15 cm) and 3" (7.5 cm) when folded.
2. Place the hatband in front of you horizontally and fold the strip in half from left to right. Unfold the band and use a pencil to lightly mark the center.
3. Cut a strip 3" x 10" (7.5 x 25 cm) from C and spray glue over base front.

ASSEMBLE

1. Using the Xs in the illustration as a guide, glue the center fan and the large arrowheads to the back of the band.
2. Glue the medium and small arrowheads to the base front.
3. To adjust the band size, follow step 4 in Headband Base Construction on page 31.

Rainbow Goddess

In Greek mythology, Iris is the goddess of rainbows, sea, and sky. She travels with the speed of wind between the gods and mortals. The word "iridescence" is, in part, derived from her name. She's often depicted as a rainbow or a girl with wings on her shoulders.

Pay close attention to the rainbow of paint swatches at your local paint store and you may learn some great lessons about color. The chips are usually arranged in order of the rainbow and how they are mixed. By mixing the primary colors—red, blue, and yellow—you can make all of the colors of the rainbow. Red + blue = purple. Blue + yellow = green. Red + yellow= orange. To make pastel colors, simply add a little white to any of these.

I made a rainbow-colored headdress, but you can explore other palette options. Possible color schemes include a fade from one color to another, such as from a deep hue to a pastel, or a combination of earth tones.

NOTE: The shape of my goddess crown resembles the headdress worn by Papua New Guinea tribes. They gather the most colorful feathers, leaves, beads, grasses, twine, bones, and fur to make tall, spectacular hats that they wear on special occasions. They have many rainbow-colored bird feathers to choose from, and they might have been the earliest upcycle artists on the planet.

{ MATERIALS }

» 48 RAINBOW-COLORED PAINT SWATCHES FOUND AT A PAINT OR HARDWARE STORE MEASURING AT LEAST 3" x 1" (7.5 x 2.5 CM)

» **A:** 9 GREEN SWATCHES, INCLUDING 1 DEEP, 2 MEDIUM DARK, 2 MEDIUM LIGHT, 2 LIGHT, AND 2 LIGHTEST

» **B:** 10 BLUE SWATCHES, INCLUDING 2 DEEP, 2 MEDIUM DARK, 2 MEDIUM LIGHT, 2 LIGHT, AND 2 LIGHTEST

» **C:** 9 VIOLET SWATCHES, INCLUDING 1 DEEP, 2 MEDIUM DARK, 2 MEDIUM LIGHT, 2 LIGHT, AND 2 LIGHTEST

» **D:** 8 RED TO PINK SWATCHES, INCLUDING 2 DEEP RED, 2 DARK PINK, 2 MEDIUM PINK, AND 2 LIGHT PINK

» **E:** 7 ORANGE SWATCHES, INCLUDING 1 DEEP, 2 MEDIUM DARK, 2 MEDIUM, 2 AND LIGHT

(continued)

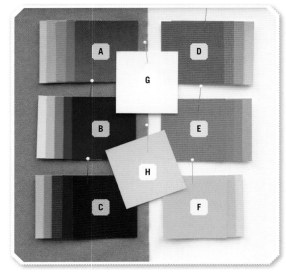

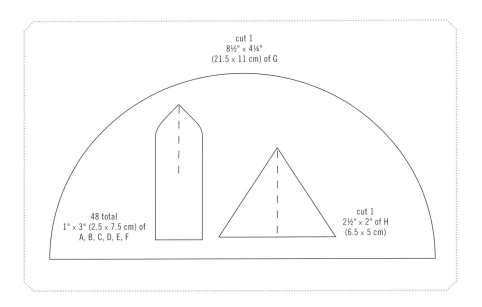

cut 1
8½" × 4¼"
(21.5 × 11 cm) of G

48 total
1" × 3" (2.5 × 7.5 cm) of
A, B, C, D, E, F

cut 1
2½" × 2" of H
(6.5 × 5 cm)

{ MATERIALS } *(continued)*

» **F:** 5 YELLOW SWATCHES, INCLUDING 1 DEEP, 2 MEDIUM, AND 2 LIGHT

» **G:** A HALF CIRCLE OF COVER WEIGHT 8½" × 4¼" (21.5 × 11 CM)

» **H:** MEDIUM YELLOW TRIANGLE, CUT FROM A PIECE OF LIGHT-WEIGHT PAPER MEASURING
2½" × 2" (6.5 × 5 CM)

» SCISSORS

» HOT GLUE GUN AND GLUE

» PENCIL

» RULER

» SEWING MACHINE

INSTRUCTIONS

RAINBOW FEATHERS

1. Using the feather template, trace and cut 48 feathers measuring 1" × 3" (2.5 × 7.5 cm), one from each color.

2. Gently fold each feather in half lengthwise at the top only, leaving the bottom flat.

3. On half circle G, use a pencil to mark every ½-inch (1.3 cm), starting 1½" (4 cm) down from the curved top. When completed, there will be six ½-inch (1.3 cm) markings.

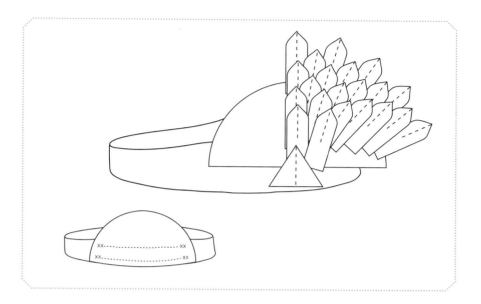

HAT BASE

1. Using a paper grocery bag, follow steps 1–3 for Headband Base Construction on page 31, making the total band height 6" (15 cm) and 3" (7.5 cm) when folded.
2. Place the hatband horizontally in front of you and fold the strip in half from left to right. Unfold the band and use a pencil to lightly mark the center.

ASSEMBLE

1. Using the Xs in the illustration as a guide, with a sewing machine, attach the half-circle G onto the center of the hatband, leaving 1" (2.5 cm) of the half-circle on either end free.
2. At the top of the half-circle, starting with green feathers and finishing with yellow feathers, glue each row of color onto the half-circle, placing the deeper colors in the center and the medium to light colors on either side. Alternate rows so each feather is arranged in between the feather in the row above and below it, with the exception of the bottom row of yellow. For that row, align center yellow feather with the center orange feather and remaining yellow feathers as shown in the photo.
3. Trim any excess feather edges that overhang the bottom edge of the hatband.
4. Glue the yellow triangle from H in center of the yellow feathers, aligning the edges with the hat base and half-circle. Fit the hat to head and glue, overlapping the band edges.
5. To adjust the band size, follow step 4 in Headband Base Construction on page 31.

Viking Warrior

The Vikings, ancient pirates from Scandinavia, explored and conquered much of the world in their long boats. They were fierce in battle and great storytellers. They worshipped a one-eyed god named Odin, who rode an eight-legged horse. His son, Thor, was the god of thunder.

Our Viking Warrior hat draws inspiration from Thor and Erik the Red, who is remembered in medieval Icelandic stories as the first Norseman of Greenland. It's believed he was a redhead, maybe with bushy eyebrows?

NOTE: Viking helmets used in battle were made of iron, and they didn't have horns on them. There's only one example of a Viking helmet in existence today, and it doesn't look very frightening. The way that we imagine the horned Viking helmet today might be because of costumes designed for an opera written by opera composer Wilhelm Richard Wagner in the 1800s.

{ MATERIALS }

- » **A:** PAPER GROCERY BAG
- » **B:** HEAVY TEXTURED WATERCOLOR PAPER
- » **C:** LIGHT BROWN COVER-WEIGHT PAPER
- » **D:** RED/BROWN RIBBED COVER-WEIGHT PAPER
- » **E:** BROWN SOFT-TEXTURED PAPER
- » **F:** RED CONSTRUCTION PAPER
- » **G:** RED/BROWN SOFT-TEXTURED PAPER
- » **H:** MOTTLED BROWN COVER STOCK
- » BROWN WATERCOLOR PAINT
- » BROWN CRAYON
- » SCISSORS
- » PENCIL
- » RULER
- » HOT GLUE GUN AND GLUE
- » PAINTBRUSH

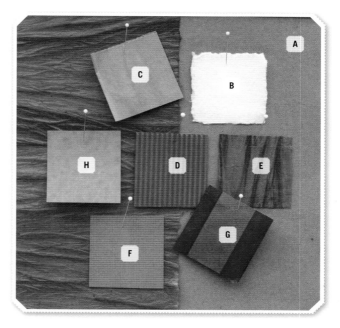

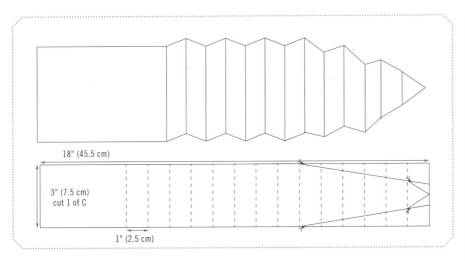

18" (45.5 cm)

3" (7.5 cm)
cut 1 of C

1" (2.5 cm)

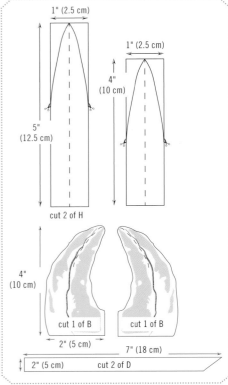

1" (2.5 cm)

1" (2.5 cm)

5"
(12.5 cm)

4"
(10 cm)

cut 2 of H

4"
(10 cm)

cut 1 of B

cut 1 of B

2" (5 cm)

7" (18 cm)

2" (5 cm)   cut 2 of D

INSTRUCTIONS

LIGHTNING BOLT

1. Cut a 3" x 18" (7.5 × 45.5 cm) strip from paper C.

2. From the right side of strip, use the diagram as a guide to trim 2 tapered wedges from the top and bottom 6" (15 cm). Trim additional small wedges to make a pointed end.

3. Starting 4" (10 cm) from the left of the lightning bolt, measure and mark 14 1" (2.5 cm) marks with a pencil. Accordian-fold at each 1" (2.5 cm) mark.

4. Glue lightning bolt onto base, matching up Xs.

HORNS

1. Using the template, trace and cut the horns from B.

2. Paint the toned areas indicated on the template with water, then dab with brown watercolor paint.

3. Blot and draw scratchy ridge with brown crayon (or watercolor crayon). Pinch and fold slightly along curved ridge to give horn dimension.

4. Cut 2 each of the small and large horn accents from H. Cut 2 each of the long thin horn accents from D. Assemble two sets that reflect each other, placing tall in center with small and large to right or left.

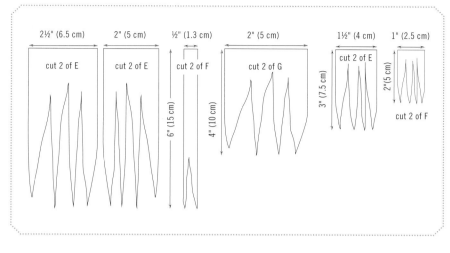

2½" (6.5 cm) 2" (5 cm) ½" (1.3 cm) 2" (5 cm) 1½" (4 cm) 1" (2.5 cm)

cut 2 of E   cut 2 of E   cut 2 of F   cut 2 of G   cut 2 of E

6" (15 cm)   4" (10 cm)   3" (7.5 cm)   2" (5 cm)

cut 2 of F

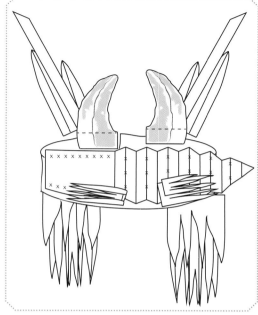

HAIR AND BROWS

1. For hair, cut 2 each from E and F. Cut 2 from G. Assemble and glue the hair at the top for left and right by putting E on bottom, F next, with G on top.

2. For brows, cut 2 each from E and F. Layer, placing E on the bottom before centering F on top. Glue. Fold over sides of E to partially cover F.

HAT BASE

1. Using paper A, follow steps 1–3 for Headband Base Construction on page 31, making the band height 6" (15 cm) and 3" (7.5 cm) when folded.

ASSEMBLE

1. Glue the lightning bolt made with C to the hat base, starting 5" (12.5 cm) from the left, using Xs to guide glue placement.

2. Glue on the horn combination, matching the glue line to the top edge of the band.

3. Glue the eyebrows onto the front of the hat and glue the hair on either side, to the back of the band.

4. To adjust the band size, follow step 4 in Headband Base Construction on page 31.

Aqua Goddess

There are many water deities in mythology and ancient civilizations. The Aztecs had Chalchiuhtlicue, the Irish worshipped Sinann, the Chinese revered Mazu, the Egyptians had Nephthys, the Finns worshipped Vedenemo, Africans had Idemili, and Greeks had too many water deities to mention.

For our water goddess, I like the idea of combining the soft, flowing texture of watercolor with the crisp, royal accents of gold.

NOTE: I chose light, bright turquoise and lavender hues, but deep, dark blues and purples can work, especially if used with copper metallic accents. For my inspiration and an accent I used a scrap booking paper by Heidi Grace Design called Beyond the Sea/Fish that has a metallic blue base with tiny gold and green fish on it.

{ MATERIALS }

» **A:** THREE STRIPS OF WHITE WATERCOLOR PAPER, MEASURING 3" x 8" (7.5 x 20.5 CM), 4" x 10" (10 x 25.5 CM), AND 5" x 12" (12.5 x 30 CM)
» **B:** 2 8½" x 11" (21.5 x 28 CM) WHITE COVER STOCK
» **C:** 8½" x 11" (21.5 x 28 CM) PATTERNED BLUE/GREEN PAPER
» **D:** 8½" x 11" (21.5 x 28 CM) METALLIC GOLD TISSUE PAPER
» **E:** 2" x 2" (5 x 5 CM) GOLD JOSS PAPER
» GREEN, BLUE, WHITE, AND PURPLE WATERCOLOR PAINTS
» PAPER GROCERY BAG
» PENCIL
» SCISSORS
» HOT GLUE GUN AND GLUE
» PAINTBRUSH
» SMOOTH ROUND DOWEL OR PENCIL

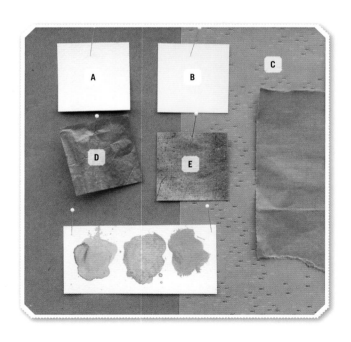

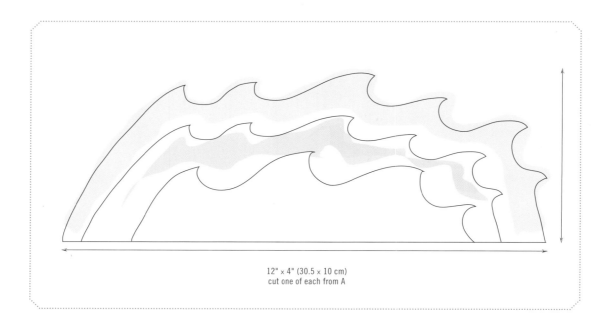

12" × 4" (30.5 × 10 cm)
cut one of each from A

INSTRUCTIONS

WAVES

1. Using the three wave templates, trace and cut out waves from watercolor paper A.

2. Mix watercolors to make a small amount of pastel blue, pastel green, and pastel lavender paints.

3. Brush the curved wave edges with water. On the large and small wave strips, paint the curved edges with pastel blue paint, allowing the color to bleed and fade to the white paper.

4. Repeat step 3 on the medium wave, using pastel green paint.

5. While the paper is still wet, splatter each wave with pastel lavender and blue paint. Set aside to dry.

CROWN FAN, SPIKES, STARFISH, AND TENDRILS

1. Using templates for spikes and starfish, trace and cut pieces from D and E after backing with B using spray glue.

2. Spray glue B on back of C then cut fan and fold according to the illustration.

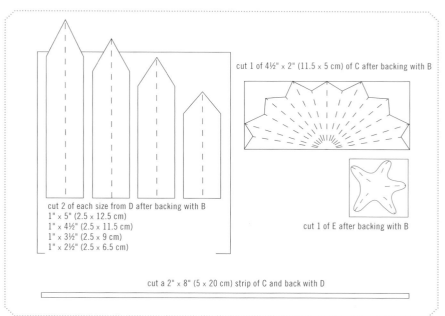

cut 1 of 4½" × 2" (11.5 × 5 cm) of C after backing with B

cut 2 of each size from D after backing with B
1" × 5" (2.5 × 12.5 cm)
1" × 4½" (2.5 × 11.5 cm)
1" × 3½" (2.5 × 9 cm)
1" × 2½" (2.5 × 6.5 cm)

cut 1 of E after backing with B

cut a 2" × 8" (5 × 20 cm) strip of C and back with D

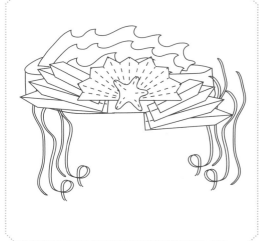

3. Cut a 2" × 8" (5 × 20 cm) strip of C, back with D, and then trim into eight ¼" × 8" (0.6 x 20 cm) strips.

4. Curl the tendrils around a smooth round pencil or dowel.

HAT BASE

1. Using a paper grocery bag, follow steps 1-3 for Headband Base Construction on page 31, making the band height 6" (15 cm) or 3" (7.5 cm) when folded.

2. Place the hatband horizontally in front of you and fold the strip in half from left to right. Unfold the band and use a pencil to lightly mark the center.

ASSEMBLE

1. Glue waves (A) to the back of the band, and fan (C), spikes (D), starfish (E), and tendrils to the front.

2. To adjust the band size, follow step 4 in Headband Base Construction on page 31.

Hairy Beast

The popular Disney movie *Beauty and the Beast* is based on a French fairytale written by Jeanne-Marie Le Prince de Beaumont who lived in the 1700s. She was a governess in London, and she wrote many stories, poems, and schoolbooks for children.

{ MATERIALS }

All of the materials I used for this design came from a recycling center or my own recycling bin. The perforated Kraft paper used for packing fragile things is one of my favorite materials to play with for hats. It can be stretched, curved, spread out, fringed, and formed in so many fun ways.

If the perforated packing material isn't available to you, I recommend using Kraft paper, cutting it into thin strips and crinkling it.

- » **A:** BROWN EGG CARTON
- » **B:** MEDIUM BROWN COVER WEIGHT PAPER
- » **C:** PERFORATED KRAFT PAPER PACKING MATERIAL
- » **D:** DARK BROWN COVER WEIGHT PAPER
- » **E:** OCHRE COVER WEIGHT PAPER
- » PAPER GROCERY BAG
- » BLACK WATERCOLOR PAINT
- » PENCIL
- » SCISSORS
- » HOT GLUE GUN AND GLUE
- » PAINTBRUSH

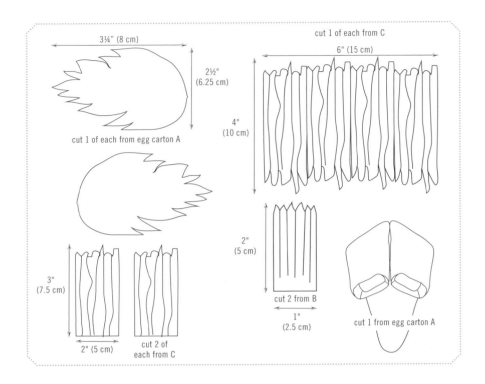

cut 1 of each from C

6" (15 cm)

4"
(10 cm)

3¼" (8 cm)

2½"
(6.25 cm)

cut 1 of each from egg carton A

3"
(7.5 cm)

2"
(5 cm)

2" (5 cm)

cut 2 of
each from C

cut 2 from B

1"
(2.5 cm)

cut 1 from egg carton A

INSTRUCTIONS

EARS, NOSE, AND HAIR

1. Trace and cut the ears from the smooth section of the egg carton A and the nostrils and nose from the lid closure.

2. Glue the nostrils to the nose.

3. Brush the ear tips and tips cut from the medium brown with black watercolor paint and set aside to dry.

4. Using nose and ear hair templates, trace and cut hair for ears from C and hair for nose from B and C.

5. Brush hair tips with black watercolor paint and set aside to dry.

HEAD HAIR

1. Using the diagrams, cut the hair from C, D, and E.

2. Cut the packing material (C) on the ends to give it a shredded appearance and cut into ½" (1.3 cm) strips, leaving 1" (2.5 cm) at the bottom.

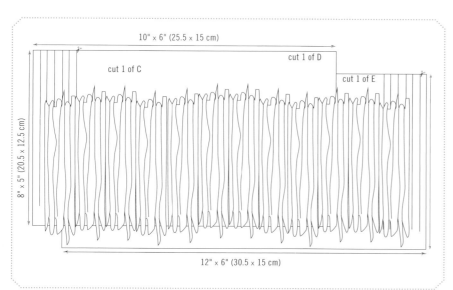

10" x 6" (25.5 x 15 cm)

cut 1 of D

cut 1 of C

cut 1 of E

8" x 5" (20.5 x 12.5 cm)

12" x 6" (30.5 x 15 cm)

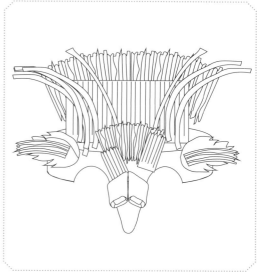

3. Cut strips as indicated for the hair from D and E. Krinkle the dark brown D strips, trim ends to points, and roll the ocher E strips.

HAT BASE

1. Using a paper grocery bag, follow steps 1–3 for Headband Base Construction on page 31, making the band height 5" (12.5 cm).

2. Place the hatband horizontally in front of you and fold the strip in half from left to right. Unfold the band and use a pencil to lightly mark the center.

3. Measure placement for the eyes and cut openings.

ASSEMBLE

1. Glue the ears, nose, and hair on where indicated.

2. To adjust the band size, follow step 4 in Headband Base Construction on page 31.

Rose Bloom

Wearing a wreath of flowers in your hair has been traditional in many cultures throughout history. A wreath of vines, flowers, and ribbons are part of the springtime maypole festival in England. The Swedish girls wear a flower headdress for midsummer festivals. In Hawaii, wearing a flower behind your left ear means you're married, and wearing one behind your right ear means you're single.

Our wreath, which is worn just above the eyebrows, includes a large, single rose with lattice and ribbons. You decide if you want the rose on the right or left.

NOTE: In Shakespeare's *Romeo and Juliet*, Juliet argues that it doesn't matter what something is named when she says, "A rose by any other name would smell as sweet." I chose the old-fashioned cabbage rose as the inspiration for this hat. The old Dutch masters loved painting them, and I love smelling them. Roses have been a favorite flower of gardeners for more than 5,000 years, long before Shakespeare ever wrote about love or roses.

{ MATERIALS }

» **A:** 5 LARGE COFFEE FILTERS
» **B AND C:** 2 CONTRASTING COVER WEIGHT BROWN PAPERS
» **D:** FLORESCENT BRIGHT GREEN PAPER
» **E:** GREEN ANTIQUE EPHEMERA
» 6" (15 CM) FLORAL WIRE
» GREEN FLORAL TAPE
» LIGHT PINK WATERCOLOR PAINT
» DEEP RED WATERCOLOR PAINT
» BRIGHT YELLOW WATERCOLOR PAINT
» PAPER GROCERY BAG
» PENCIL
» SCISSORS
» PAINTBRUSH
» HOT GLUE GUN AND GLUE
» SPRAY GLUE
» PINKING SHEARS

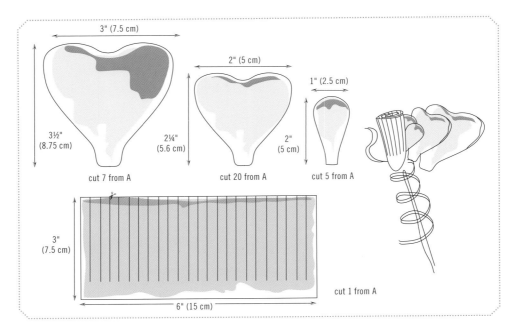

3" (7.5 cm)

3½"
(8.75 cm)

2¼"
(5.6 cm)

cut 7 from A

2" (5 cm)

2"
(5 cm)

cut 20 from A

1" (2.5 cm)

cut 5 from A

3"
(7.5 cm)

6" (15 cm)

cut 1 from A

INSTRUCTIONS

PETALS

1. Using the petal templates, trace and cut 7 large, 20 medium, and 5 small petals from A.
2. Using watercolors, paint the petals a light pink. While the petals are still wet, brush a little deep red on outer edges of a few large, medium, and small petals, letting the red bleed into the pink. Set aside to dry.

STAMEN

1. Using the stamen template, trace and cut stamen from A.
2. Paint with bright yellow watercolor.
3. Make a bright orange paint by mixing a little deep red with a lot of bright yellow and brush tips of stamen while it's still wet. Set aside to dry.

ROSE

1. When stamen is dry, tightly roll and glue the unfringed end to make a little bunch.
2. Holding the fringed stamen end, insert about 1 inch (2.5 cm) of the floral wire into the stamen and tightly wrap the floral tape around the unfringed end of the stamen. Continue wrapping down to the bottom of the wire and repeat 3 times.

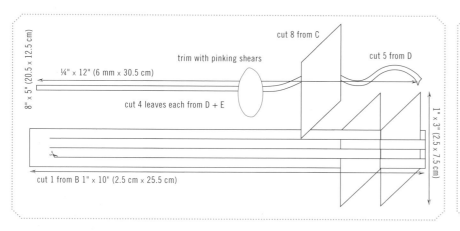

8" x 5" (20.5 x 12.5 cm)

cut 8 from C

trim with pinking shears

cut 5 from D

¼" x 12" (6 mm x 30.5 cm)

cut 4 leaves each from D + E

1" x 3" (2.5 x 7.5 cm)

cut 1 from B 1" x 10" (2.5 cm x 25.5 cm)

3. Starting with the smallest petals, glue the petals around the base of the stamen, overlapping slightly until all of the petals are attached. Wrap the stem and base of the rose tightly 2 times with the floral wire.

LATTICE
1. Cut the lattice base from B, leaving ½" (1.3 cm) uncut at one end and 8 strips from B.
2. Weave the angled strips in and out of the lattice base and slide the strips all the way to the left, leaving no gaps between the angles, and glue.

LEAVES AND VINES
1. Using the leaf templates, trace and cut 4 leaves each from D and E.
2. Carefully trim the outer edges with the pinking shears, making the E leaves smaller. Glue small leaves on top of large leaves. Cut thin vine strips from the florescent bright green paper D and curl the strips around a smooth, round pencil.

HAT BASE
1. Using grocery bag, follow steps 1-4 for Headband Construction on page 31, making the band height 6" (15 cm) or 3" (7.5 cm) when folded.
2. Place the hatband horizontally in front of you and fold the strip in half from left to right. Unfold the band and use a pencil to lightly mark the center.

ASSEMBLE
1. Glue lattice to center front of hat band. Tuck leaf and vine ends and vines into lattice and glue.
2. Coil the rose stem and glue rose to front side of band.

Dragonfly

When I was little, I was afraid of these beautiful bugs. They looked sinister to me then, but they are harmless and actually help us by eating mosquitoes. Dragonflies need to live near ponds or rivers where they can lay their eggs. There are more than 5,000 species of dragonflies, and some can fly as fast as 38 miles (61 km) per hour. In prehistoric times, huge dragonflies buzzed around dinosaurs.

NOTE: The dragonfly is often used as a design motif in fabric, pottery, silverware, and wallpaper. There is even a British motorcycle named after the bug. They are used often in the work from the Art Nouveau movement.

My inspiration for this hat was the colors and patterns found in wallpaper from the early 1900s. The psychedelic 1960s might be another source of inspiration. I started the design with a Kraft paper bag with avocado printing on one side. Most of the other papers came from a recycling center I go to often.

{ MATERIALS }

- » **A:** AVOCADO GREEN PAPER
- » **B:** COPPER METALLIC PAPER
- » **C:** PURPLE TISSUE PAPER
- » **D:** BROWN COVER-WEIGHT PAPER
- » **E:** TEAL AND PURPLE MARBLEIZED PAPER
- » **F:** METALLIC GOLD AND LAVENDER TISSUE PAPER
- » PAPER GROCERY BAG
- » PENCIL
- » SCISSORS
- » HOT GLUE GUN AND GLUE

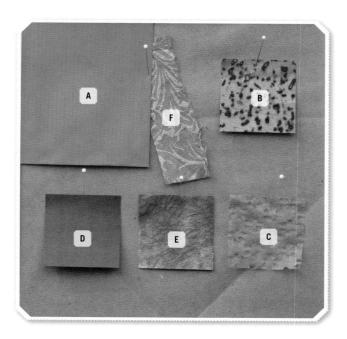

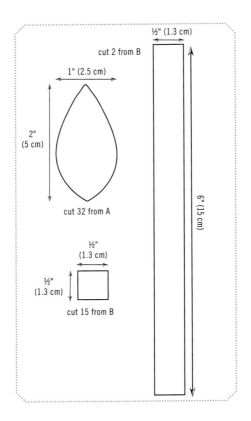

½" (1.3 cm)

cut 2 from B

1" (2.5 cm)

2"
(5 cm)

6" (15 cm)

cut 32 from A

½"
(1.3 cm)

½"
(1.3 cm)

cut 15 from B

INSTRUCTIONS

LEAVES, BUDS, AND BAND

1. Using the leaf template, cut 32 leaves from A. Because the paper is thin, fold a strip in two, trace the leaves, and cut two at a time.

2. From B, cut 15 small square buds and two bands for either side of hat.

BUG PARTS

1. Using the templates, trace and cut the bug parts from B, C, D, E, and F.

HAT BASE

1. Using a paper grocery bag, follow steps 1–3 for Headband Base Construction on page 31, making the band height 2" (5 cm), or 1" (2.5 cm) when folded.

2. Place the hatband horizontally in front of you and fold the strip in half from left to right. Unfold the band and use a pencil to lightly mark the center.

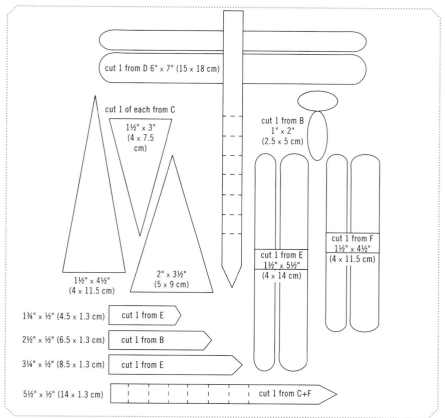

cut 1 from D 6" x 7" (15 x 18 cm)

cut 1 of each from C

1½" x 3"
(4 x 7.5 cm)

cut 1 from B
1" x 2"
(2.5 x 5 cm)

1½" x 4½"
(4 x 11.5 cm)

2" x 3½"
(5 x 9 cm)

cut 1 from E
1½" x 5½"
(4 x 14 cm)

cut 1 from F
1½" x 4½"
(4 x 11.5 cm)

1¾" x ½" (4.5 x 1.3 cm) cut 1 from E

2½" x ½" (6.5 x 1.3 cm) cut 1 from B

3¼" x ½" (8.5 x 1.3 cm) cut 1 from E

5½" x ½" (14 x 1.3 cm) cut 1 from C+F

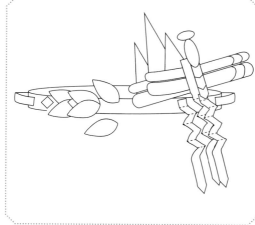

ASSEMBLE

1. Beginning from the left, 10" (25 cm) from the center and continuing to the right, alternate overlap of leaves, keeping the leaf ends centered top to bottom on band.
2. Glue the buds between the leaves and the bands on either side of the leaves.
3. Assemble the dragonfly as shown, gluing to the front of the band, to the right of center.
4. Cut the lavender wedges from C and glue them behind the dragonfly to the inside of the hat band.
5. To adjust the band size, follow step 4 in Headband Base Construction on page 31.

CHAPTER 3

Folded HATS

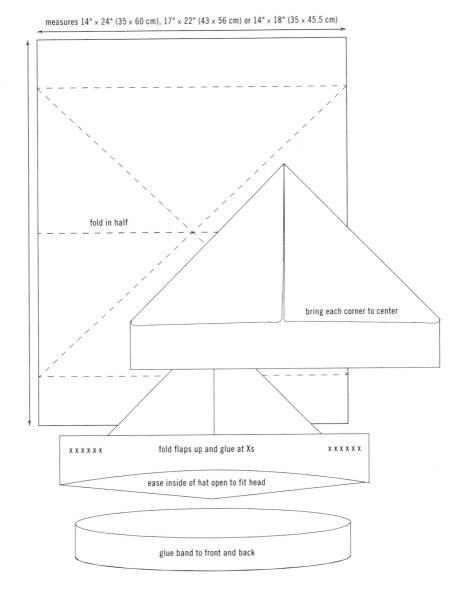

measures 14" x 24" (35 x 60 cm), 17" x 22" (43 x 56 cm) or 14" x 18" (35 x 45.5 cm)

fold in half

bring each corner to center

x x x x x x   fold flaps up and glue at Xs   x x x x x x

ease inside of hat open to fit head

glue band to front and back

{ MATERIALS }

» **A:** NEWSPAPER, OR ANY OTHER PAPER WITH MULTIPLE LAYERS OR A COVER-WEIGHT PAPER LIKE WALLPAPER OR A PAPER GROCERY BAG, CUT TO ONE OF THE FOLLOWING SIZES:
  ◦ ROBIN HOOD: 14" x 24" (35 x 60 CM)
  ◦ DUTCH GIRL: 17" x 22" (43 x 56 CM)
  ◦ PIRATE: 14" x 18" (35 x 45.5 CM)

» **B:** COVER-WEIGHT STOCK FOR INSIDE BAND

» RULER

» HOT GLUE GUN AND GLUE

» SPRAY GLUE

Folded Hat Construction

FITTING

For this book, the models ranged in age from two to twelve years old, with head circumferences between 20" (51 cm) and 23" (58.5 cm). This design includes a hatband made to fit each head exactly, and it's glued inside the folded hat at the front and back.

CUTTING AND FOLDING

1. Cut A to the correct size for the project you are making. If the newspaper or grocery bag is not large enough, use two pieces adhered together with a seam of masking tape.
2. To make hat, place A in front of you vertically and fold in half, bringing the bottom edge of the paper up to meet the top edge.
3. Mark the centerline by folding the paper in half again, this time bringing the left edge of the paper across to meet the right edge. Unfold and allow the paper to lay flat in front of you.
4. Fold the lower right corner up to meet the centerline then fold the lower left corner up to meet the centerline.
5. Fold a 2" (5 cm) flap of paper at top down to cover top of corners.
6. Flip the hat over and fold a 2" (5 cm) flap to match the flap on the opposite side.
7. Apply glue to the inside of the flaps as indicated by the Xs on the diagram.
8. Ease the inside of the hat open to fit head.

CLOSURE

1. Measure B to the head, overlap the edges, and glue to size.
2. Insert the band inside the hat, making sure that most of it is concealed. Glue the band to the inside front and back of the hat.
3. Glue the flaps together in front and on ends.

Robin Hood

The story of Robin Hood has been told for more than 800 years. Early ballads, Maypole celebrations, books, and films have presented many different versions of this lovable outlaw who stole from the rich and gave to the poor. A skilled archer with a great sense of humor, Robin Hood had the uncanny ability to hide from his enemy in broad daylight. Today Robin Hood's tale can provide inspiration for hours of fun play in the woods.

NOTE: Because Robin Hood is at times brash and bold and other times he needs to disappear into tree branches, I've designed the hat with both leaves for camouflage and bright red feathers that yell "come and get me!"

{ MATERIALS }

- » **A:** 14" x 24" (35 x 60 CM) AND 4" x 24" (10 x 60 CM) PAPER GROCERY BAGS
- » **B:** 7¾" x 7¼" (19.5 x 18.5 CM) LIGHT-WEIGHT KRAFT PAPER
- » GREEN, RED, YELLOW, ORANGE, BROWN, AND BLACK WATERCOLOR PAINTS
- » LIGHT GREEN, BRIGHT RED, AND BROWN WATERCOLOR OR REGULAR CRAYONS
- » 36" (91.5 CM) PIECE NATURAL BROWN GARBAGE TWINE OR RAFFIA
- » PENCIL
- » SCISSORS
- » PINKING SHEARS
- » HOT GLUE GUN AND GLUE
- » SINGLE HOLE PUNCH
- » PAINTBRUSH

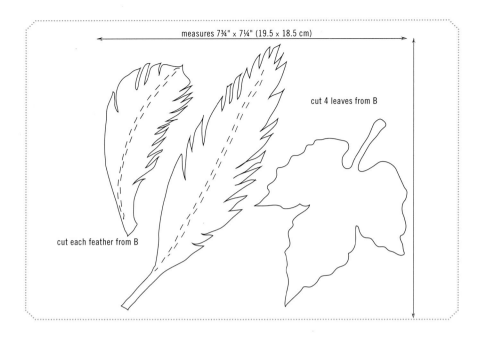

measures 7¾" x 7¼" (19.5 x 18.5 cm)

cut 4 leaves from B

cut each feather from B

INSTRUCTIONS

LEAVES AND FEATHERS

1. Using the template, trace and cut 4 leaves from B.

2. Lightly dab green, red, yellow, and brown watercolors on the leaves to create a mottled effect. Set aside to dry.

3. Once the leaves have dried, use the light green crayon to draw leaf veins. With the red crayon, outline some of the leaf tips.

4. Using the two feather templates, trace and cut feathers from paper B.

5. Paint the feathers red with orange accents. Set aside to dry.

6. Once the feathers are dry, use the brown crayon to draw a center ridge, veins, and tips on each feather. Use the bright red crayon to draw accents and highlights.

7. Gently crease the centers of the leaves and the feathers. The creases on the leaves should be concave and the creases on the feathers should be convex.

RAWHIDE

1. Dab the garbage twine or raffia with brown watercolor paint. Set aside to dry.

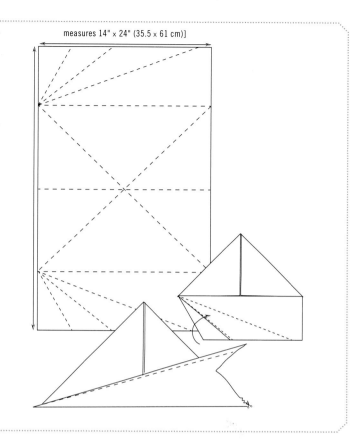

measures 14" x 24" (35.5 x 61 cm)]

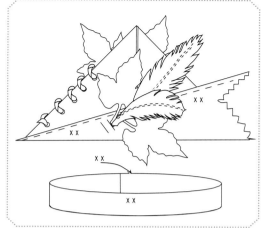

HAT BASE

1. Trace and cut the hat base from A.

2. Follow the directions in Folded Hat Construction on page 67. The hat sides on this hat are slightly different, folding up at an angle to better resemble Robin Hood's hat. Fan folding three times from one edge, fold brims at an angle so the brim at front is as narrow as possible. Create a crease ⅛" (3 mm) in front and ending at ½" (1.3 cm) at back. Using a pinking shears, cut a wedge from the wide edge of the brim to resemble the illustration.

3. Measure the head and cut a band from B that is 2" (5 cm) longer than head measure and 4" (10 cm) wide, 2" (5 cm) when folded.

4. Fold band in half along its length, overlap edges to fit, and glue.

ASSEMBLE

1. Use a hole punch to make 5 holes for twine where indicated on illustration.

2. Paint brown-black eyelets around the lace holes and set aside to dry.

3. Lace the garbage twine or raffia through the holes. Dab black-brown paint on the ends of the garbage twine near the eyelets.

4. Use a craft knife to cut a slit for the feathers, slip in the feathers and glue secure. Trim back the edge of the hat flaps with pinking shears and glue the hat brim edges on Xs.

5. Glue the band to inside of hat at the Xs.

Dutch Girl

This hat was inspired by the Dutch, specifically by their love of tulips and their tradition of making beautiful Delft blue ceramic tiles. The pretty blue and white paper came from an outdated wallpaper book. The wallpaper in these books is strong, and two pages taped together are the perfect size for a folded hat. I added a band of paper inside to better secure it to a child's head.

NOTE: I added a little touch of white lace by using a die cutter from the craft store, but a paper doily would work just as well. I also enlarged the tulip pattern and made a bouquet for the model to hold.

{ MATERIALS }

» **A:** 12" x 12" (30.5 x 30.5 CM) RED AND WHITE POLKA DOT PAPER

» **B:** 12" x 12" (30.5 x 30.5 CM) YELLOW AND WHITE FLORAL PAPER

» **C:** TWO 12" x 12" (30.5 x 30.5 CM) SHEETS COMPLIMENTARY GREEN-PATTERNED PAPER

» **D:** TWO 11" x 17" (28 x 43 CM) SHEETS BLUE AND WHITE WALLPAPER BOOK PAGES (ONE WON'T SHOW.)

» **E:** TWO 3" x 16" (7.5 x 40 CM) BLUE AND WHITE COMPLIMENTARY WALLPAPER PAGES

» **F:** TWO 2" x 12" (5 x 30 CM) STRIPS OF BLUE AND WHITE CHECKED PAPER

» **G:** 2" x 24" (5 x 61 CM) STRIP WHITE COVER STOCK

» **H:** 8" x 3" (20.5 x 7.5 CM) STRIP WHITE PAPER CUT WITH LACE DIE-CUTTER OR TWO SMALL DOILIES

» TWO 10" (25.5 CM) PIECES CLOTH-COVERED FLORAL WIRE

» HOT GLUE GUN AND GLUE

» SPRAY GLUE

» PENCIL

» SCISSORS

» MASKING TAPE OR WHITE ART TAPE

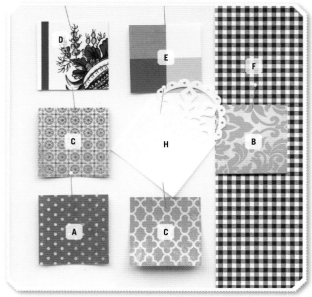

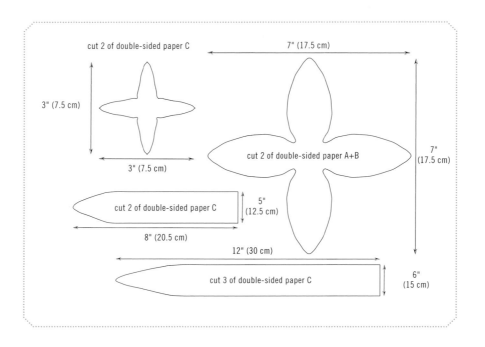

cut 2 of double-sided paper C

3" (7.5 cm)

3" (7.5 cm)

7" (17.5 cm)

7" (17.5 cm)

cut 2 of double-sided paper A+B

cut 2 of double-sided paper C

5" (12.5 cm)

8" (20.5 cm)

12" (30 cm)

cut 3 of double-sided paper C

6" (15 cm)

INSTRUCTIONS

TULIPS

1. Apply spray glue to the back of A and attach the glued side to the back of B, smoothing out the air bubbles from the center to the edges.
2. Trace one tulip pattern on the red paper side (A) and one on the yellow paper side (B), then cut out both.
3. Repeat step 2, using the smaller, flower bottom template and two leaf templates on the two green-patterned papers (C).
4. Using a small, sharp pair of scissors carefully poke a small hole in the smaller tulip base and slide it onto the floral wire. Then poke a small hole in the larger tulip center and push floral wire through hole, pushing the larger flower center on top of the smaller flower base. Bend the top ½" (1.3 cm) of wire at a right angle inside the tulip bloom. Cut a ½" (1.3 cm) square from the tulip paper (A or B) and glue on top of the bent wire, to hide the wire and secure the flower. Slide the tulip bottom up to the flower base and glue the two pieces together. Score, fold, and glue the insides of leaves, sandwiching the end of the wire in between.

HAT BASE

1. Place the two pages from the wallpaper book (D) wrong-side-up on a work surface, aligning so that two of the 17" (43 cm) sides meet.
2. Use masking tape to adhere these two sides together, creating one large piece of wallpaper measuring 22" × 17" (56 × 43 cm).
3. Following the directions in Folded Hat Construction on page 67, fold D into a hat.

ATTACH DECORATIVE BAND

1. Spray glue strips (E) to front and back of up-turned hat flaps.
2. Hot glue ends of flaps together.

ASSEMBLE

1. Apply spray glue to back side of checkered paper (F) and adhere to white cardstock (G).
2. Measure the band to the head, overlap the edges, and glue to size.
3. Insert the band inside the hat, making sure most of it is concealed. Glue the band to the inside front and back of the hat.
4. Die-cut a lace pattern from white paper or cut a doily in half (H).
5. First glue the doilies then the flowers to the hat, tucked just inside the front brim.
   Optional: Construct a colorful bouquet of tulips to create a pretty complement to the hat.

Pirate

Transform yourself from a landlubber into a true buccaneer in three easy steps. The first and most important step is to make this fun hat. Then begin each sentence with "ARRRR" and use "me" instead of "I."

NOTE: If a black and white map isn't available, it's always fun to make your own treasure map that's personalized for your adventure.

{ MATERIALS }

» **A:** 14" x 18" (35 x 45 CM) BLACK AND WHITE MAP OR HAND-DRAWN MAP
» **B:** ONE 2" X 14" (5 X 35 CM) AND TWO 3" X 24" (7.5 X 60 CM) PIECES ANTIQUED, HANDWRITTEN NOTE PAPER
» **C:** 2" x 24" (5 x 61 CM) STRIP WHITE COVER STOCK
» **D:** 4" x 4" (10 X 10 CM) DARK BROWN AND BLACK PATTERNED PAPER
» **E:** 4" x 4" (10 x 10 CM) BLACK PAPER
» 12" (30 CM) RED AND WHITE BAKER'S TWINE
» PALE BLUE AND BROWN WATERCOLOR PAINTS
» WHITE, RED, AND BLACK CRAYONS
» RULER
» PENCIL
» SCISSORS
» PAINTBRUSH
» WOODEN MATCHES
» TRACING PAPER
» LARGE DARNING NEEDLE
» SINGLE HOLE PUNCH
» HOT GLUE GUN AND GLUE

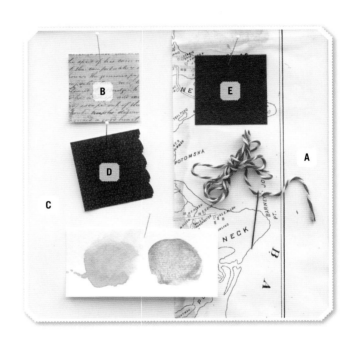

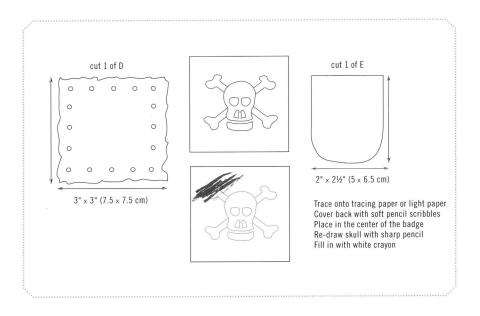

cut 1 of D

3" x 3" (7.5 x 7.5 cm)

cut 1 of E

2" x 2½" (5 x 6.5 cm)

Trace onto tracing paper or light paper
Cover back with soft pencil scribbles
Place in the center of the badge
Re-draw skull with sharp pencil
Fill in with white crayon

INSTRUCTIONS

HAT BASE

1. Measure and cut the hat base from purchased map or hand-drawn map (A).

2. Follow the directions for Folded Hat Construction on page 67.

3. As shown in photo, lightly paint water areas with pale blue watercolor paint and lightly paint land areas with pale brown watercolor paint, then set aside to dry.

4. To make the headband, fold 3" (7.5 cm) strips of (B) in half and spray glue to cover stock (C).

5. Fit the band to head and glue closed.

6. When the hat base is dry, fold along the dotted lines and burn the front flap edge. Do this a few inches at a time, blowing out and lighting a new match as you go. Tuck in the back flap on the sides and glue.

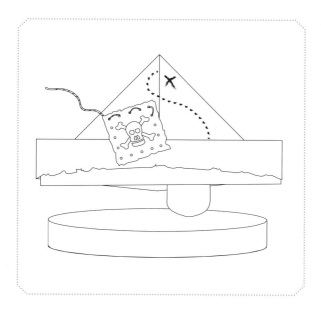

BADGE AND PATCH

1. Cut the badge from the patterned paper (D), trim the edges to look rough, transfer the skull, and fill it in with white crayon. Using a single hole punch, cut holes as indicated on the illustration.

2. Trace and cut the eye patch from the black paper (E).

ASSEMBLE

1. Glue the third single handwritten strip (B) under the front flap so it peeks out between the burned edges of the hat front.

2. Glue the band to the front and back of the hat inside.

3. Align the badge to the front of the hat and sew on with the red and white bakers twine, using a large darning needle.

4. Align the patch with the eye and glue it to the band inside the hat.

5. With black and red crayon, draw a dotted line, an x, and an arrow to show where the treasure is buried.

CHAPTER 4

Cone HATS

measures 10¼" × 7½" (25.6 × 19 cm); enlarge to 10" (25 cm) high for large size, for small size reduce to 5¾" (14.4 cm)

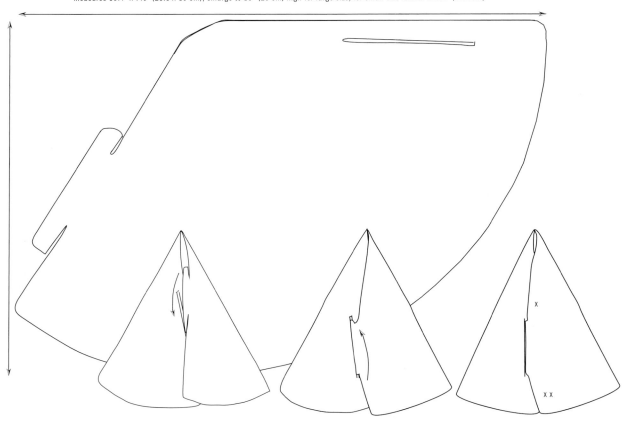

Cone Hat Base Construction

This hat is meant to be a base that will be covered with decorative paper, so the color doesn't matter as long as there's no show through.

{ MATERIALS }

» COVER STOCK PAPER

» SCISSORS

» HOT GLUE

INSTRUCTIONS

CUTTING AND ASSEMBLY

1. Trace and cut the hat shape using the template, taking care to cut the slit and around the curved tabs.

2. Spray the mount cover paper that's called for in the specific pattern to the hat base, burnishing from the center out to smooth any air bubbles. Trim cover paper to edges. Roll the hat base to soften for assembly. Slide the bottom tab in first, from the top down. Push the tab into the slot from right to left and up. Smooth out any creases and apply hot glue where indicated by Xs.

Sticky-Note Stinky Bug Hat

Our bug isn't exactly a stink bug, but because it's made out of fluorescent office supplies, it's a hard hat to ignore. An office supply store can be an inspiring source for hat materials, and the bright orange sticky notes I found became the ingredient upon which I based everything else. You might have all of these materials in your home office supply closet and kitchen pantry.

NOTE: Saying Sticky Stinky Bug five times fast might be harder than making this hat. This design was made as a small-size hat.

{ MATERIALS }

» **A:** TWO 8½" x 11" (21.5 x 28 CM) SHEETS GREEN FLUORESCENT COVER-WEIGHT PAPER
» **B:** 8½" x 11" (21.5 x 28 CM) FLUORESCENT TURQUOISE COVER-WEIGHT PAPER
» **C:** TWO 3" x 3" (7.5 x 7.5 CM) FLUORESCENT ORANGE STICKY NOTES
» **D:** ONE 6" x 8" (15 x 20.5 CM) PIECE UNBLEACHED PARCHMENT BAKING PAPER
» **E:** 8½" x 11" (21.5 x 28 CM) WHITE CARD STOCK
» **F:** TWO WHITE PAPER TAGS WITH METAL TRIM
» 14" (35.5 CM) ROUND WHITE ELASTIC CORD, MEDIUM WEIGHT
» PENCIL
» SCISSORS
» HOT GLUE GUN AND GLUE
» SPRAY GLUE

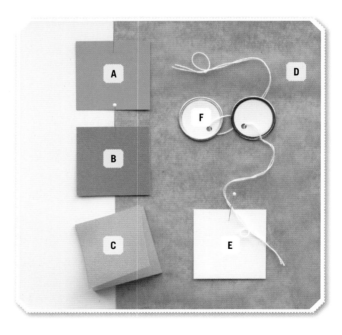

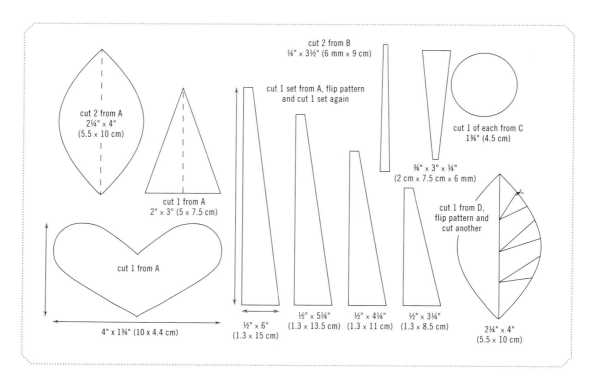

cut 2 from B
¼" × 3½" (6 mm × 9 cm)

cut 1 set from A, flip pattern
and cut 1 set again

cut 2 from A
2¼" × 4"
(5.5 × 10 cm)

cut 1 of each from C
1¾" (4.5 cm)

¾" × 3" × ¼"
(2 cm × 7.5 cm × 6 mm)

cut 1 from A
2" × 3" (5 × 7.5 cm)

cut 1 from D,
flip pattern and
cut another

cut 1 from A

4" × 1¾" (10 × 4.4 cm)

½" × 6"
(1.3 × 15 cm)

½" × 5¼"
(1.3 × 13.5 cm)

½" × 4¼"
(1.3 × 11 cm)

½" × 3¼"
(1.3 × 8.5 cm)

2¼" × 4"
(5.5 × 10 cm)

INSTRUCTIONS

BUG PARTS

1. Using the templates, trace and cut the wings, head, legs, and belly for the bug from the fluorescent green paper (A) and spray glue to turquoise paper (B).

2. Working from the center out, smooth any bubbles and trim the excess paper.

3. Trim the sticky edge from the orange sticky notes (C), and then trace and cut the bug nose and outer eyes.

4. Trace and cut out the antennae from the turquoise paper (B). Trace and cut out the wing overlays from the parchment paper (D) and fold in half.

HAT BASE

1. Using the small cone hat template, follow directions for Cone Base Construction on page 83, using white card stock (E).

2. Spray glue green paper (A) on the hat base, trim and push any bubbles from center out, to smooth.

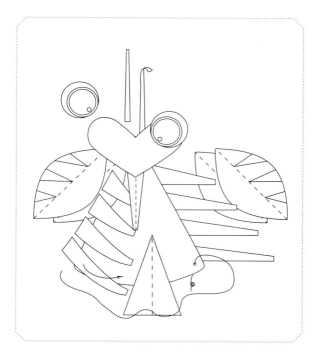

3. Follow the directions for assembly on page 83.

4. Lightly draw a pencil line from the top to the bottom on the hat base front, which is exactly opposite to where the hat edges join.

ASSEMBLE

1. Glue the leg backs to the hat back, aligning the edges with the hat edges and placing the leg tips in front.

2. Folding the belly triangle in half, align it with the center pencil mark on the hat and glue on top of the leg tips in the front of the hat.

3. Fold the bug head and nose in half, glue the outer and center eyes, antennae, and nose to the head, aligning with the center belly crease.

4. Glue the wings onto the top back of the base, angling them out. Using a pair of small, sharp scissors, carefully poke small holes in hat on the sides (¾" [2 cm] up from the bottom), measure the elastic, and thread through the holes.

5. Place the hat on the head and triple knot the ends of the elastic to fit.

Wee Bunny

Velveteen, Calico, Easter: Who doesn't love a little bunny? This rabbit definitely evokes a sense of spring, when baby bunnies are most abundant. To sit better on a little head, I made this hat proportionately smaller and put plenty of interest in back for when that little bunny hops away.

I added a lot of small pattern to this hat in spring green and lavender to softly contrast with the bright white. Chocolate brown and yellow or light brown and pink are wonderful color combinations, too. You can find many origami or scrapbook papers with tiny patterns, which would be just right for this design.

NOTE: This design was made as a medium-size hat.

{ MATERIALS }

- » **A:** 8½" x 11" (21.5 x 28 CM) WHITE CARD STOCK
- » **B:** 9" X 12" (22.5 X 30 CM) SHEET OF WHITE AND LAVENDER PRINT COVER PAPER
- » **C:** 3" X 3" (7.5 X 7.5 CM) SHEET OF SOLID LAVENDER COVER PAPER
- » **D:** 6" X 6" (15 X 15 CM) SHEET OF GOLD AND GREEN PATTERNED PAPER
- » **E:** GREEN AND WHITE ORIGAMI PAPER
- » **F:** 4" X 4" (5 X 5 CM) SHEET OF WHITE VELLUM PAPER
- » 14" (35.5 CM) ROUND WHITE ELASTIC CORD, MEDIUM WEIGHT
- » PENCIL
- » SCISSORS
- » HOT GLUE GUN AND GLUE
- » SPRAY GLUE
- » DECORATIVE EDGE SCISSORS

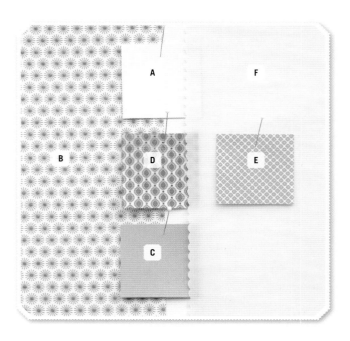

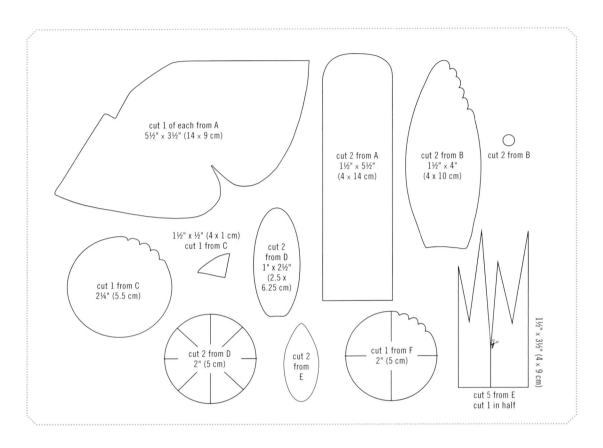

cut 1 of each from A
5½" x 3½" (14 x 9 cm)

cut 2 from A
1½" x 5½"
(4 x 14 cm)

cut 2 from B
1½" x 4"
(4 x 10 cm)

cut 2 from B

1½" x ½" (4 x 1 cm)
cut 1 from C

cut 2
from D
1" x 2½"
(2.5 x
6.25 cm)

cut 1 from C
2¼" (5.5 cm)

cut 2 from D
2" (5 cm)

cut 2
from
E

cut 1 from F
2" (5 cm)

1½" x 3½" (4 x 9 cm)

cut 5 from E
cut 1 in half

INSTRUCTIONS

HAT BASE

1. Using the medium size template, follow the directions for Cone Base Construction on page 83, using white cover stock (A).

2. Spray glue the printed lavender paper (B) onto the base, trim, and push any bubbles from the center out, to smooth.

3. Follow the directions for assembly on page 83.

BUNNY

1. Trace and cut the bunny face and arms from A, the ears and eyes from B, and the nose from C. Trace and cut the tail from C and F.

2. Glue the inner ears to the outer ears, the eyes and the nose to the face, and the tail top to the tail bottom. Fold in the ear ends to make a flat surface to glue and attach the ears to the head.

FLOWERS AND GRASS

1. Trace and cut the flower parts from C and D and the leaves from E.

2. Using decorative edge scissors, trim the edges of the flower circles from C and F as shown in the photo.

3. Glue the flowers and leaves together.

ASSEMBLE

1. Glue the grass to the hat bottom, leaving the tips unglued.

2. Assemble the head in the same way as the hat, gluing the back edge. Glue the head and arms to the hat base and the ears to the head. Glue the bunny tail and flower onto the back, tucking them behind the top of the grass blades.

3. Using a pair of small, sharp scissors, carefully poke small holes in the hat on each side, ¾" (2 cm) from the edge, measure the elastic, and thread through the holes.

4. Place the hat on the head and triple knot the ends of the elastic to fit.

Magician's Assistant

I performed a magic act at school events when I was eleven and twelve years old. A book from the library, a cape, and a few props were all I needed to create the show that dazzled my audience. This hat would have been great to keep my audience focused away from my hands, where all the magic needed to happen.

NOTE: Magicians traditionally wear top hats where they can hide their rabbits or birds. I designed this hat with a wizard's hat in mind, which gives you a lot of space to display magical shapes and accents. This design was made as large-size hat.

{ MATERIALS }

Most of the papers for this hat are from a recycling center. The matte and shiny papers make this design more interesting. The contrast of neutral-colored papers with accents of orange, green, and silver add visual play and drama.

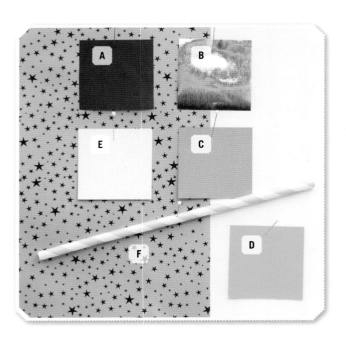

- » **A:** TWO 8½" x 11" (21.5 x 28 CM) SHEETS OF MATTE DARK BLUE PAPER
- » **B:** 8½" x 11" (21.5 x 28 CM) SHEET OF METALLIC SILVER
- » **C:** 8½" x 11" (21.5 x 28 CM) SHEET OF BRIGHT ORANGE PAPER
- » **D:** 8½" x 11" (21.5 x 28 CM) SHEET OF BRIGHT GREEN PAPER
- » **E:** 12" x 16" (30 x 40.5 CM) SHEET OF WHITE COVER STOCK
- » **F:** 12" x 16" (30 x 40.5 CM) SHEET OF PATTERNED GREY PAPER
- » 1 LIGHT BLUE STRIPED PAPER STRAW
- » 14" (35.5 CM) ROUND WHITE ELASTIC CORD, MEDIUM WEIGHT
- » SPRAY GLUE
- » PENCIL
- » SCISSORS
- » CRAFT KNIFE
- » HOT GLUE GUN AND GLUE

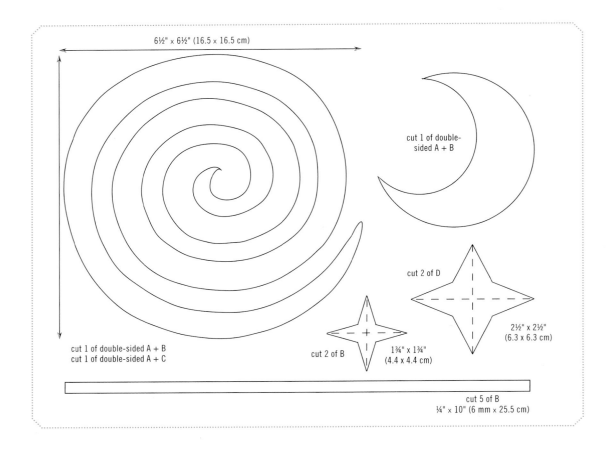

6½" x 6½" (16.5 x 16.5 cm)

cut 1 of double-sided A + B

cut 2 of D

cut 2 of B

1¾" x 1¾"
(4.4 x 4.4 cm)

2½" x 2½"
(6.3 x 6.3 cm)

cut 1 of double-sided A + B
cut 1 of double-sided A + C

cut 5 of B
¼" x 10" (6 mm x 25.5 cm)

INSTRUCTIONS

ACCENTS

1. Spray glue one sheet of the dark blue paper (A) to the back of the silver paper (B) and spray glue the other sheet of the dark blue paper (A) to the back of the orange paper (C), smoothing out any bubbles from the center to the outer edges.

2. Trace the spiral template onto the double-sided silver and orange papers and cut.

3. Trace and cut out the silver stars (B) and the green stars (D). Fold as shown.

4. Cut the strips of paper from D and crimp ½" (1.3 cm) folds.

5. Trace and cut the moon from double-sided A + B. Cut the straw, to about 5" (12.5 cm), notch the end ½" (1.3 cm), and slide the moon into the notch

HAT BASE

1. Trace the large cone hat template onto white cover stock (E) and cut it out.

2. Spray glue the gray patterned paper (F) to the white cover stock, trim, and push any bubbles from the center out to smooth.

3. Follow the directions for assembly on page 83.

ASSEMBLE

1. Using a craft knife, 3" (7.5 cm) from the top, carefully cut a ½" (1.3 cm) X on the side of the hat and slide the straw through the hole, leaving 4" (10 cm) of the straw above the hole.

2. Hot glue the straw on both the inside and the outside.

3. Attach the green strips and spirals as shown.

4. Using a pair of small, sharp scissors, carefully poke small holes in the hat on the sides, measure the elastic, and thread it through the holes.

5. Place the hat on the head and triple knot the ends of the elastic to fit.

Butterfly Peek-A-Boo

I have a garden planted for butterflies and hummingbirds to play. The flowers and grass are tall and colorful. As the summer tapers into fall, it seems the hummingbirds speed up and the butterflies slow down.

NOTE: You can also make an additional oversized butterfly and attach it to a ribbon for your child to flutter on her finger. This design was made as a medium-size hat.

{ MATERIALS }

I chose a summer yellow and sky blue palette for this hat. Other options might be rainbow hues or soft earthy colors; Lots of variations on white could be pretty too.

» **A:** 8½" x 11" (21.5 x 28 CM) SHEET WHITE CARD STOCK
» **B:** 8½" x 11" (21.5 x 28 CM) SHEET LIGHT BLUE POLKA DOT PAPER
» **C:** 4 WHITE MINI CUPCAKE LINERS
» **D:** 3 SOFT YELLOW PAPER PAINT CHIPS
» **E:** 2 CREAM PAINT CHIPS
» **F:** 16 SOFT GREEN PAINT CHIPS, 4 EACH OF DARKER, MEDIUM, LIGHT, AND VERY LIGHT HUES
» 14" (35 CM) ROUND WHITE ELASTIC CORD, MEDIUM WEIGHT
» HOT GLUE GUN AND GLUE
» SPRAY GLUE
» PENCIL
» SCISSORS

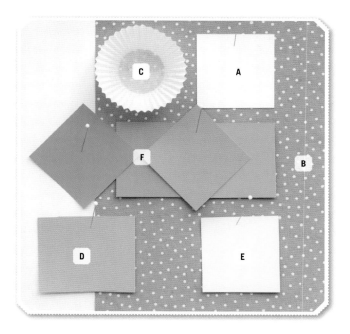

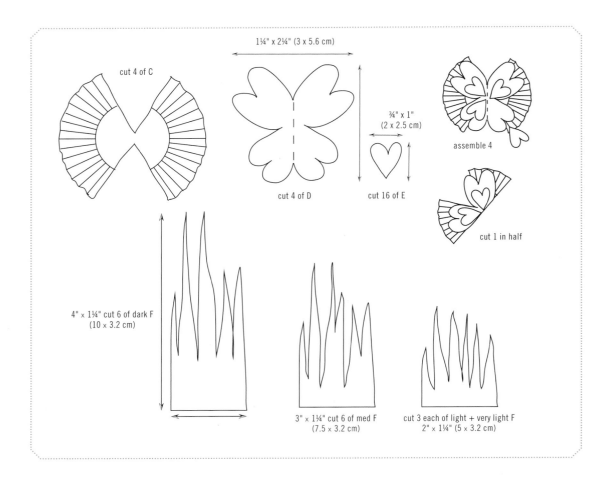

cut 4 of C

1¼" x 2¼" (3 x 5.6 cm)

cut 4 of D

¾" x 1"
(2 x 2.5 cm)

cut 16 of E

assemble 4

cut 1 in half

4" x 1¼" cut 6 of dark F
(10 x 3.2 cm)

3" x 1¼" cut 6 of med F
(7.5 x 3.2 cm)

cut 3 each of light + very light F
2" x 1¼" (5 x 3.2 cm)

INSTRUCTIONS

HAT BASE

1. Using the template, cut a cone hat from white cover stock (A).

2. Spray glue the blue paper (B) to the white cover stock, trim, and push any bubbles from the center out to smooth.

3. Follow the directions for assembly on page 83.

BUTTERFLIES AND GRASS

1. Trim "V" shapes from the top and sides of the cupcake liners (C).
2. Cut the yellow (D) and cream parts (E) for the wings.
3. Assemble four butterflies and cut one butterfly into two halves.
4. Use the grass templates to trace and cut the grass strips from (F).

ASSEMBLE

1. Using the illustration as a guide, glue the grass to the hat bottom, staggering the greens and placing shorter grass in front of taller blades.
2. Trim any excess edges from the curved hat bottom.
3. Glue on the butterflies as shown in the illustration.
4. Using a small, sharp scissors, carefully poke small holes in the hat on the sides, measure the elastic, and thread it through the holes.
5. Place the hat on the head and triple knot the ends of the elastic to fit.

SSSSSnake

Snakes always seem a little on the sneaky side to me. They surprise me in my garden and woodpile and even sometimes on my porch steps. The snake on this hat doesn't stand a chance of being sneaky because it's made out of the double-sided fluorescent paper I found at a craft store.

NOTE: If these colors make you reach for sunglasses and you prefer a more subtle snake, try using finely patterned origami papers. Using pages from an old gardening catalogue for scales would give a snake a lot of places to hide. This design was made as a medium-size hat.

{ MATERIALS }

- » **A:** 8½" x 11" (21.5 x 28 CM) WHITE COVER STOCK
- » **B:** 8½" x 11" (21.5 x 28 CM) SHEET DARK ORANGE FLUORESCENT PAPER
- » **C:** 8½" x 11" (21.5 x 28 CM) SHEET LIGHT ORANGE FLUORESCENT PAPER
- » **D:** 8½" x 11" (21.5 x 28 CM) SHEET YELLOW AND PINK DOUBLE-SIDED FLUORESCENT PAPER
- » **E:** 8½" x 11" (21.5 x 28 CM) SHEET GREEN FLUORESCENT PAPER
- » **F:** 5" x 5" (12.5 x 12.5 CM) DULL BLACK PAPER
- » 14" (35 CM) ROUND WHITE ELASTIC CORD, MEDIUM WEIGHT
- » PENCIL
- » SCISSORS
- » HOT GLUE GUN AND GLUE
- » SPRAY GLUE

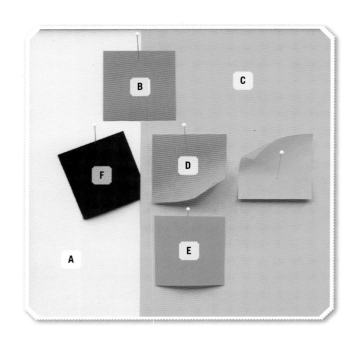

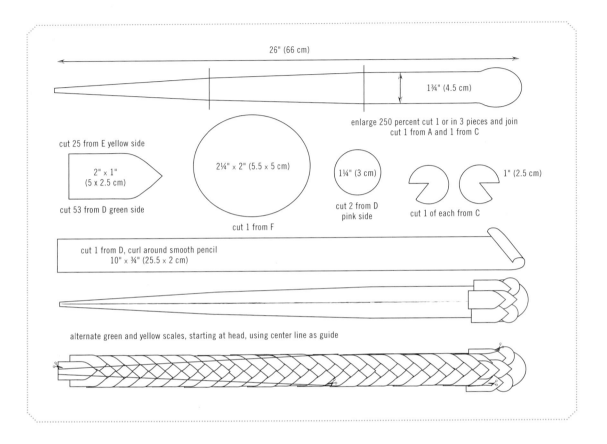

26" (66 cm)

1¾" (4.5 cm)

enlarge 250 percent cut 1 or in 3 pieces and join
cut 1 from A and 1 from C

cut 25 from E yellow side

2" x 1"
(5 x 2.5 cm)

2¼" x 2" (5.5 x 5 cm)

1¼" (3 cm)

1" (2.5 cm)

cut 53 from D green side

cut 2 from D
pink side

cut 1 of each from C

cut 1 from F

cut 1 from D, curl around smooth pencil
10" x ¾" (25.5 x 2 cm)

alternate green and yellow scales, starting at head, using center line as guide

INSTRUCTIONS

HAT BASE

1. Using the small cone hat template, cut a hat base from the white cover stock (A).

2. Spray glue the orange paper (B) to the white cover stock base, trim, and push any bubbles from the center out to smooth.

3. Follow the directions for assembly on page 83.

SNAKE BODY, EYES, AND TONGUE

1. Using the template, cut the snake body from cover stock (A).

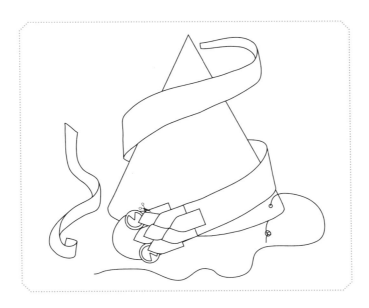

2. Spray glue the snake body onto the orange paper (C), trim, and push any bubbles from the center out to smooth.

3. Trace and cut the eyes and tongue from the light orange and pink papers (C and D).

4. Trace and cut 25 yellow/pink scales from paper (E) and 53 green scales from paper (D).

5. Trace and cut the head from the dull black paper (F).

6. Glue the head to the wide end of the snake's body on the white cover stock side, and then draw a light pencil line down the center of the snake's back. Use the pencil line as a guide for gluing on the scales, starting at the head and working to the end of the tail. As the tail tapers in size, trim the outside edges of the scales that overhang the body base.

7. Assemble the eyes and glue the eyes to the snake face.

8. Glue the tongue to the back of the snake's head. Roll the tongue on a smooth round dowel or pencil to curl. Gently curl the tips of the scales with your fingertips, curling up and back.

ASSEMBLE

1. Glue the snake's head and tail where indicated on the front bottom and top of the hat.

2. Using a pair of small, sharp scissors, carefully poke small holes in the hat on the sides, measure the elastic, and thread it through the holes.

3. Place the hat on the head and triple knot ends to fit.

CONE HATS

CHAPTER 5

Brim HATS

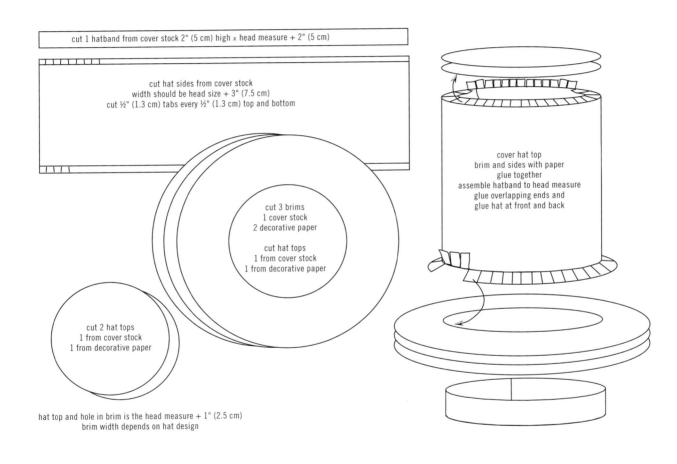

cut 1 hatband from cover stock 2" (5 cm) high × head measure + 2" (5 cm)

cut hat sides from cover stock
width should be head size + 3" (7.5 cm)
cut ½" (1.3 cm) tabs every ½" (1.3 cm) top and bottom

cut 3 brims
1 cover stock
2 decorative paper

cut hat tops
1 from cover stock
1 from decorative paper

cut 2 hat tops
1 from cover stock
1 from decorative paper

cover hat top
brim and sides with paper
glue together
assemble hatband to head measure
glue overlapping ends and
glue hat at front and back

hat top and hole in brim is the head measure + 1" (2.5 cm)
brim width depends on hat design

Brim Hat Construction

This will be a base that decorative paper will adhere to so color doesn't matter, as long as there's no show through.

{ MATERIALS }

» COVER STOCK PAPER
» PENCIL
» SCISSORS
» SPRAY GLUE
» HOT GLUE GUN AND GLUE

INSTRUCTIONS

CUTTING AND ASSEMBLY

1. Trace and cut the parts for the base and decorative covers, using the measuring directions in the illustration.
2. Spray glue the decorative papers called for in the specific pattern to the hat top, brim top, and sides. Burnish well.
3. Carefully trim the decorative paper to cover the stock tabs, leaving the tabs bare.
4. Bring the sides of the hat together and hot glue to create a cylinder.
5. Fold the tabs on the top of the hat in and fold the bottom tabs out.
6. Hot glue the hat top to tabs, 3 to 4 tabs at a time, carefully working your way around the hat, keeping the folded ends flush with the hat top edge. Slide the brim down the hat cylinder to rest on top of tabs.
7. Flip the hat over and hot glue, keeping the tab edges tight to the inside edge of the brim. Glue the underside brim cover over brim to conceal the glued tabs.
8. Fit the band to the head, cover and glue together with decorative paper, and glue closed. Glue the hatband to hat inside front and back, hiding most of the band inside the hat.

Mad Hatter

Our crazy top hat is based on the fur top hats worn two and three centuries ago. In the 1800s, when hat makers made hats from fur, they might have inhaled fumes that often lead to a terrible sickness. Nervousness, extreme shyness, shakiness, and confused speech were symptoms of "Mad Hatters Disease." Lewis Carroll, the author of *Alice's Adventures in Wonderland*, grew up in a town where hat making was the main occupation. Many believe the hatter Carroll wrote about in his book was inspired by the "mad hatters" he knew growing up.

NOTE: The first top hat was worn by a hat maker, John Hetherington, in 1797. It was rumored to have caused a near riot. A newspaper stated "passersby panicked at the sight. Women fainted, children screamed, dogs yelped, and an errand boy's arm was broken when he was trampled by the mob." Mr. Hetherington was brought to court and charged for wearing "a tall structure having a shining luster calculated to frighten timid people."

MATERIALS

I chose a color scheme of contrasting colors. Another color scheme that's equally fun and crazy could be neons or black, white, and red.

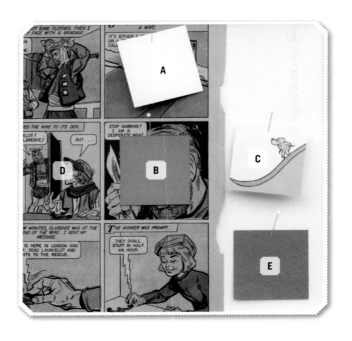

- » **A:** WHITE COVER-WEIGHT PAPER (8" [20.5 CM] x HEAD MEASURE + 3" [7.5 CM])
- » **B:** ONE 14" x 14" (35 x 35 CM) SHEET BRIGHT ORANGE TEXT-WEIGHT PAPER
- » **C:** ONE 8½" x 11" (21.5 x 28 CM) COLORFUL PAGE FROM AN OLD STORYBOOK
- » **D:** 3 COLORFUL PAGES FROM AN OLD COMIC BOOK
- » **E:** 1 SHEET GREEN CONSTRUCTION PAPER
- » PENCIL
- » SCISSORS
- » RULER
- » SPRAY GLUE
- » HOT GLUE GUN AND GLUE

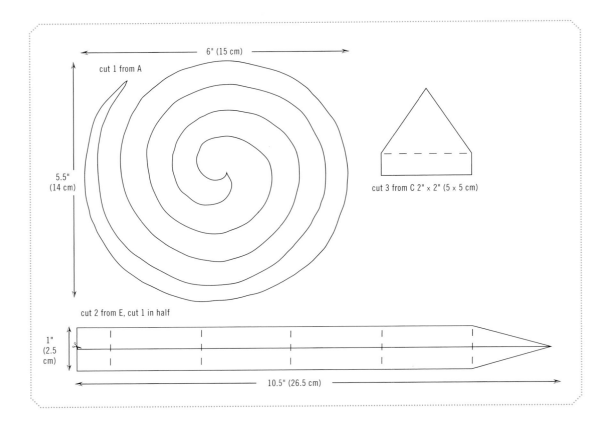

6" (15 cm)

cut 1 from A

5.5"
(14 cm)

cut 3 from C 2" x 2" (5 x 5 cm)

cut 2 from E, cut 1 in half

1"
(2.5
cm)

10.5" (26.5 cm)

INSTRUCTIONS

HAT BASE

1. Using white cover-weight paper (A), cut out the parts for the brim hat base following the directions on page 107. The brim should be a 13" (33 cm) circle and the sides should be 7" (18 cm) high without the tabs.

2. Spray glue 1 side of the brim to 1 orange paper (B), smooth from the center out and trim.

3. Spray glue the hat top to the storybook page (C), smooth from the center out and trim.

4. Spray glue the comic book pages (D) on an angle to the hat sides. Trim the pages to where the clipped edges begin on the top and bottom.

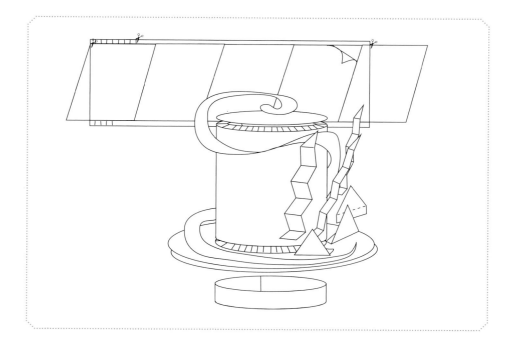

HAT ACCENTS

1. Using the spiral template, trace and cut out the spiral from the white cover paper (A).

2. Trace and cut the green lightning bolts from the green paper (E) and fold where indicated on the illustration.

3. Trace, cut, and fold the accent arrows from the old book page (C).

ASSEMBLE

1. Using the hat base guide, glue the hat edges together, hat top to side and side to brim.

2. Glue the spiral, lightning bolts, and arrows to the hat where indicated.

3. Glue the brim liner over the hat tabs.

4. Measure the inside hatband to the head, mark, and glue. Glue the band inside hat at the front and back.

Sunflower

The young sunflower, one of my favorite flowers to grow, starts each day facing a rising sun and ends each evening leaning toward the setting sun.

With a happy, brown velvet face, this hat works especially well when worn by someone with brown hair.

NOTE: The tallest sunflower recorded grew in the Netherlands to 25 feet (7.6 m) tall. Some of my favorite varieties of sunflowers are Indian Basket, Velvet Queen, Moonwalker, Moulin Rouge, Sunbright, Little Becka, and the tallest of all, American Giant.

{ MATERIALS }

I had some bright yellow crepe paper left over from a birthday party that had the perfect texture for the sunflower petals on this hat.

- » **A:** 1 ROLL YELLOW CREPE PAPER
- » **B:** FOUR 8½" x 11" (21.5 x 28 CM) SHEETS GREEN PAPER + 1 SHEET MEASURING 13" x 13" (33 x 33 CM)
- » **C:** FOUR 8½" x 11" (21.5 x 28 CM) SHEETS LIGHT KRAFT PAPER + 1 STRIP 2" (5 CM) x HEAD MEASURE + 2" (5 CM)
- » **D:** 13" x 13" (33 x 33 CM) SHEET WHITE COVER STOCK
- » **E:** 13" x 13" (33 x 33 CM) SHEET DARK BROWN PAPER
- » **F:** 13" x 13" (33 x 33 CM) SHEET RIBBED BROWN PAPER
- » PENCIL
- » SCISSORS
- » PINKING SHEARS
- » SPRAY GLUE
- » HOT GLUE GUN AND GLUE

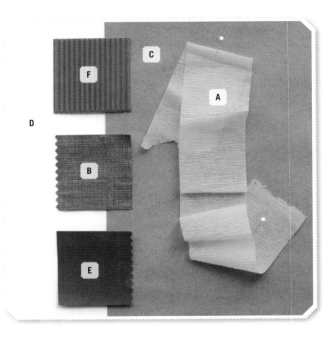

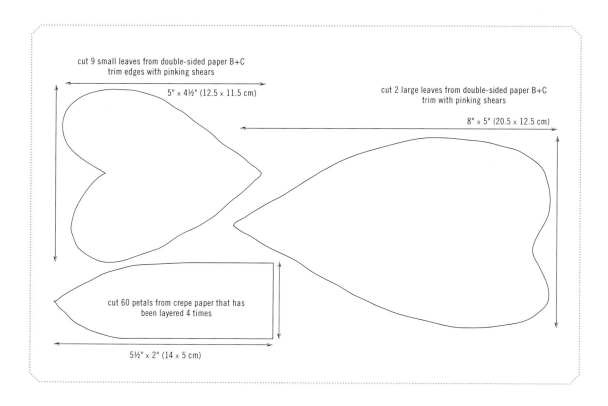

cut 9 small leaves from double-sided paper B+C
trim edges with pinking shears

5" x 4½" (12.5 x 11.5 cm)

cut 2 large leaves from double-sided paper B+C
trim with pinking shears

8" x 5" (20.5 x 12.5 cm)

cut 60 petals from crepe paper that has
been layered 4 times

5½" x 2" (14 x 5 cm)

INSTRUCTIONS

FLOWER PARTS

1. Layer the crepe paper (A) four times. Using the petal template, cut 60 petals from the crepe paper, resulting in 240 petals.

2. Assemble the petals in layers of two, dab with dot of hot glue at the base of each pair of petals, squeeze and flatten the edge to create a slightly dimensional petal.

3. Spray glue the green paper (B) onto Kraft paper (C) and burnish.

4. Trace the large and small leaves from B+C, cut, and trim all around with pinking shears.

HAT BASE

1. Cut the band from Kraft paper (C), adding three tabs on the sides and front, measure on head for fit and glue closed, leaving the tabs free.

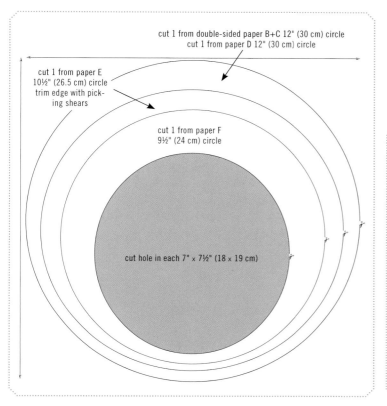

cut 1 from double-sided paper B+C 12" (30 cm) circle
cut 1 from paper D 12" (30 cm) circle

cut 1 from paper E
10½" (26.5 cm) circle
trim edge with pick-
ing shears

cut 1 from paper F
9½" (24 cm) circle

cut hole in each 7" x 7½" (18 x 19 cm)

2. Using the template, cut out the brim from white cover stock (D), spray glue to the green paper (B), and trim the outer and inner edges.

3. Attach the band to the base, gluing the tabs to the top of the white base.

ASSEMBLE

1. Starting ½" (1.3 cm) from the outer edge, glue the double-layered petals to the top of the brim and then another row, alternating the placement with the first row.

2. Cut another brim from the dark brown paper (E) and with pinking shears, trim the edge.

3. Glue the dark brown paper brim on top of the petals, tabs, and bottom brim.

4. Cut the flower center from the ribbed paper (F) and glue in place.

5. Glue the petals to underneath the brim and curl with your fingertips up and back so the petals face down.

Can O'Worms

"Don't open that can of worms" is a saying most people date back to the 1950s, when fishermen bought cans of worms for live bait. As you can imagine, once you open that can filled with worms, it's very difficult to keep all those wigglers inside.

NOTE: Did you know that earthworms are really great to have in garden soil? All the wiggling and tunneling they do loosens the soil, making it easier for plants to grow strong roots. Growing earthworms in a bin filled with moist newspaper is a fun and easy way to create compost. You can find information online on how to set up a composting worm farm at school or home.

{ MATERIALS }

I liked the colors I found in the Sunday funnies, and I used them as inspiration for this hat. Lots of pinks, baby blues, lavenders, and greens made the pink worms and silver can look especially nice. My silver paper was a great find at the recycling center, and the comics came right out of the corner market's paper dumpster.

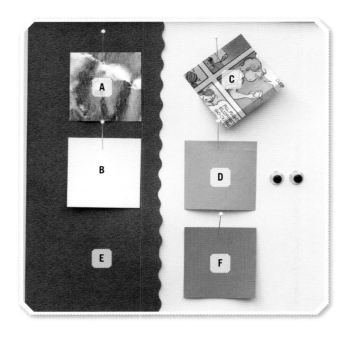

- » **A:** ONE 10" x 26" (25.5 x 66 CM) SHEET SILVER PAPER AND TWO 10" x 10" (25.5 x 25.5 CM) SHEETS SILVER PAPER
- » **B:** ONE 10" x 26" (25.5 X 66 CM) SHEET WHITE COVER-WEIGHT PAPER AND TWO 10" x 10" (25.5 x 25.5 CM) SHEETS WHITE COVER-WEIGHT PAPER
- » **C:** 2 PAGES NEWSPAPER COMICS
- » **D:** ONE 10" x 10" (25.5 x 25.5 CM) SHEET PINK PAPER
- » **E:** TWO 10" x 13" (25.5 x 33 CM) SHEETS BLACK COVER STOCK
- » **F:** ONE 3" x 2" (7.5 x 5 CM) SHEET ACID GREEN PAPER
- » TWENTY 20.5 MM GOOGLY EYES
- » CLOTH-COVERED FLORAL WIRE
- » PENCIL

(continued)

THE PAPER HAT BOOK

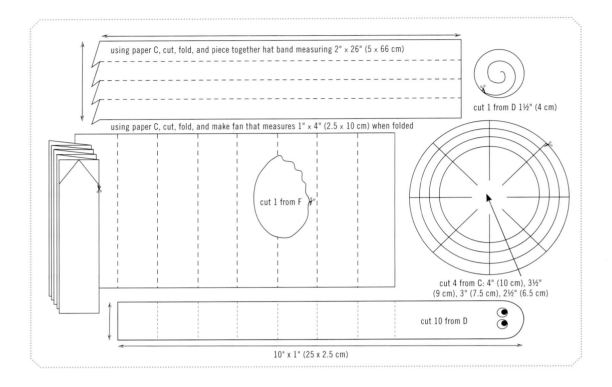

using paper C, cut, fold, and piece together hat band measuring 2" × 26" (5 × 66 cm)

cut 1 from D 1½" (4 cm)

using paper C, cut, fold, and make fan that measures 1" × 4" (2.5 × 10 cm) when folded

cut 1 from F

cut 4 from C: 4" (10 cm), 3½" (9 cm), 3" (7.5 cm), 2½" (6.5 cm)

cut 10 from D

10" × 1" (25 × 2.5 cm)

{ MATERIALS } *(continued)*

» SCISSORS

» RULER

» SPRAY GLUE

» HOT GLUE GUN AND GLUE

» DECORATIVE SCISSORS

INSTRUCTIONS

HAT ACCENTS

1. Cut, fold, and glue comic paper (C) to make a continuous hatband that measures the length of the hat.

2. Trace and cut the flowers and fan from (C) and the flower center from (D).

3. Cut the leaf from paper (F) and assemble the flower.

4. Cut 10 worms from paper (D), crimp, and glue on the googly eyes.

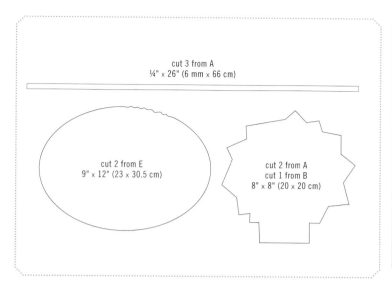

cut 3 from A
¼" x 26" (6 mm x 66 cm)

cut 2 from E
9" x 12" (23 x 30.5 cm)

cut 2 from A
cut 1 from B
8" x 8" (20 x 20 cm)

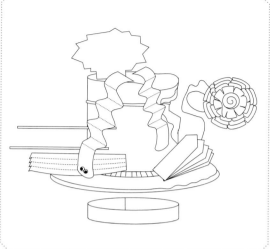

HAT BASE

1. Using the template, trace and cut out the parts for the hat from white cover-weight paper (A). The finished hat sides should be 8" (20.5 cm) tall × 26" (66 cm) wide with tabs only on the bottom.

2. Spray glue the silver paper (A) to one side of the hat top, trim, and repeat on the other side.

3. Cut and glue the ribs to the side of the hat according to the illustration.

4. Spray glue the silver paper (B) to the sides and top, smooth from the center out and trim.

5. Press out the air along the ribs to create the look of an aluminum can.

6. Spray glue the silver paper (A) to one side of the hat top, trim, and repeat on the other side.

7. Trace and cut the hat brim and 9" × 12" (23 x 30.5 cm) liner from E.

ASSEMBLE

1. Glue the hat sides together and to the brim. Glue the tab on top of the hat to the inside of the hat on the opposite side of the dented area.

2. Create dented can look by crushing one side down toward the brim.

3. Using the illustration as a guide, glue the worms to the inside of the hat and outside to give the appearance that they are escaping.

4. Glue the fan accent to the side of the brim.

5. Using a pair of small, sharp scissors, cut a small hole behind the fan, insert the flower wire, bend the end, and glue it inside the hat. Glue the brim liner over the hat tabs. Trim the edges with decorative scissors.

6. Measure the hat band to the head, add 2" (5 cm) for overlap, fit to head, and glue. Glue the inside band tabs to inside the hat sides.

BRIM HATS

Garden Fence

The delicate and faded print fabrics in antique quilts from the 1930s and 40s were my inspiration for this hat. I love how the small patterns in pinks, blues, and yellows and the weathered fence work with the shape of this hat.

{ MATERIALS }

The picket fence is made from the back side of a cereal box brushed with white watercolor paint, the grass came from an outdated wallpaper book, and the flowers are made from scrapbook paper purchased at a craft store.

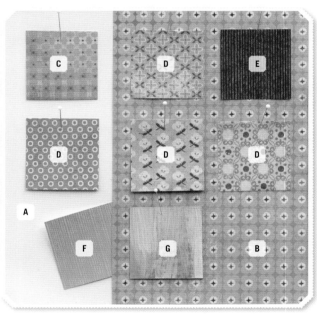

» **A:** 26" x 4" (66 x 10 CM) WHITE COVER-WEIGHT PAPER
» **B:** 12" x 12" (30 x 30 CM) YELLOW PRINTED PAPER
» **C:** 12" x 12" (30 x 30 CM) CORNFLOWER BLUE PRINT PAPER
» **D:** TWO 7" x 7" (17.5 x 17.5 CM) SHEETS PINK PRINT PAPER AND TWO 7" x 7" (17.5 x 17.5 CM) BLUE PRINT PAPERS
» **E:** 4" x 4" (10 x 10 CM) AND 12" x 12" (30 x 30 CM) DARK GREEN WALLPAPER
» **F:** 12" x 12" (30 x 30 CM) LIGHT GREEN PAPER
» **G:** LIGHTWEIGHT CEREAL OR CRACKER BOX, OPENED AND FLATTENED
» TWO 6" (15 CM) PIECES AND ONE 4" (10 CM) PIECE CLOTH-COVERED FLORAL WIRE
» WHITE WATER-BASED PAINT
» PENCIL
» RULER
» SCISSORS
» SPRAY GLUE
» PINKING SHEARS
(continued)

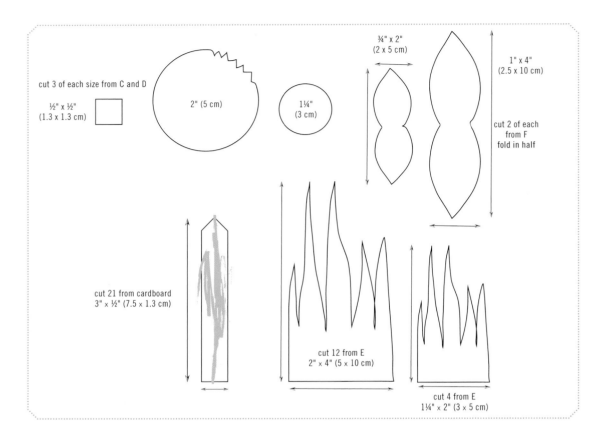

cut 3 of each size from C and D

½" x ½"
(1.3 x 1.3 cm)

2" (5 cm)

1¼"
(3 cm)

¾" x 2"
(2 x 5 cm)

1" x 4"
(2.5 x 10 cm)

cut 2 of each
from F
fold in half

cut 21 from cardboard
3" x ½" (7.5 x 1.3 cm)

cut 12 from E
2" x 4" (5 x 10 cm)

cut 4 from E
1¼" x 2" (3 x 5 cm)

{ MATERIALS } *(continued)*

» PAINTBRUSH

» HOT GLUE GUN AND GLUE

INSTRUCTIONS

HAT BASE

1. Following the directions on page 107, cut out the parts for the brim hat base. The brim should be a 12" (30 cm) circle, and the sides should be 3½" (8.75 cm) high without the tabs.
2. Spray glue the yellow paper (B) to the top side of the brim, smooth from the center out, and trim.

3. Cut the blue print (C) in 3½" x 12" (8.75 x 30 cm) strips to cover the hat sides, spray glue to cover stock (A), smooth from the center out, and trim.

4. Spray glue the blue print paper (D) to the hat top, smooth from the center out, and trim.

FLOWERS, FENCE, AND GRASS

1. Spray glue the pink papers (D) to the back of the blue papers (C), trace the flower parts using the templates, and trim with pinking shears.

2. Trace and cut the leaves from (F). Assemble the flowers on wire with leaves.

3. With a dry brush dipped in the white paint, paint the back of the cereal box (G), leaving brush marks and some cardboard showing through. Set aside to dry.

4. Trace and cut the grass from the dark green paper (E).

5. When the cereal box is dry, cut 21 pickets from cardboard.

ASSEMBLE

1. Cut the bottom brim liner from light green paper (F).

2. Using the hat base guide, glue the hat edges together, the hat top to side and the side to brim.

3. Glue the brim liner over the hat tabs on the underside of the brim.

4. Measure the inside hatband to head, mark, and glue. Glue the band inside hat at the front and back.

5. Use hot glue to attach the grass, pickets, and flowers.

Resources

There might be a recycling center near you that sells all kinds of recycled paper products at a very reduced rate. The one I go to is specifically for teachers.

Recycling for Rhode Island Education is an amazing organization, family run, and is located at 95 Hathaway St, Providence, RI.

Irecycle, an app for the iPhone that locates recycled goods and recycled centers near you, can be purchased through itunes.apple.com.

There are plenty of online sources for purchasing new and unusual papers.
www.acmoore.com
www.demedicimingfinepaper.com
www.dickblick.com
www.etsy.com
www.flaxart.com
www.japanesepaperplace.com
www.jerrysartarama.com
www.katespaperie.com
www.khadi.com
www.michaels.com
www.nycentralart.com
www.paper-source.com
www.pearlriver.com
www.utrechtart.com

About the Photographer

Paul Clancy is a self-taught artist and photographer who has enjoyed a successful commercial career for more than thirty years. Clancy's client list has included Levis, Polaroid, Audi USA, Nature's Way, Fidelity Investments, Vail/Keystone Resorts, Rockport, Saucony, Sylvania, Blue Cross, and Hewlett Packard.

Clancy has participated in an artist-in-residence program in Balatonfured, Hungary, was an artist-in-residence at AS220 and a co-teacher at Broad Street Studio's Photographic Memory program in Providence, Rhode Island. His work has been featured in *ArtScope, Providence Phoenix, Graphis, Archive,* and *Photo District News.* For more information about Paul's work, contact him at paulclancy.mail@verizon.net.

About the Author

Alyn Carlson is a New England–based graphic designer, painter, performer, paper artist, and part-time chicken rancher. In the past three decades, she has been a street performer in California, renovated a church into a home, and been the artistic producer for three theater companies. She also writes a blog called *Colorgirl.* Her designs and art have been featured in numerous blogs and published in magazines such as *Uppercase, Print, Redbook, Communication Arts, Photo District News,* and *RI Monthly.* Her paintings are featured in Deborah Forman's book *Paint Lab,* and her home appears in Grace Bonney's *Design Sponge at Home.* Alyn's art, design, and hat shop can be found at alyncarlson.com.

Paul and Alyn have collaborated on many commercial projects over the past thirty years and on several fine art projects over the past decade. On more than one occasion, Paul has modeled hats for Alyn.

Acknowledgments

THANK YOU TO

Michael Thibeault, for believing in my hats and finding a way.

Mary Ann Hall, Renae Haines, and Heather Godin for being saints with all of my questions and angst.

Ava, Brenna, Chetan, Crispin, Grace, Isaiah, Joseph, Julia, Kayla, Levi, Lila, Lucy, Massimo, Nora, Ritief, Sammy, Spencer, Violetta, Wallace, and Zoe, without you, my hats wouldn't have had a head to rest on.

Suzanne, the goddess of Photoshop.

Alan and Dottie Carlson, for teaching me how to see beauty and for the agile hands I have.

Hillary, Cameron, Brindalyn, and Alex for loving the messes their mom makes.

Kimmy, my Theo.

Barbara, Gayle, and Pat for saying, "Of course you can write a book!"

Paul Clancy, my partner in art, work, and life, for always making everything we do together look beautiful.